Fernanda Cirino

#DigitalMarket: The influence of the new consumer profile

Fernanda Cirino

#DigitalMarket: The influence of the new consumer profile

An analysis of the work of communication agencies in Belém do Pará

ScienciaScripts

Imprint

Cover image: www.ingimage.com

This book is a translation from the original published under ISBN 978-620-2-18175-4.

Publisher:
Sciencia Scripts
is a trademark of
Dodo Books Indian Ocean Ltd. and OmniScriptum S.R.L publishing group

120 High Road, East Finchley, London, N2 9ED, United Kingdom
Str. Armeneasca 28/1, office 1, Chisinau MD-2012, Republic of Moldova, Europe
Printed at: see last page
ISBN: 978-620-7-31846-9

DEDICATION

I dedicate this work to all my friends and family who have supported and encouraged me throughout my project.

TABLE OF CONTENTS

ACKNOWLEDGMENTS

I would like to thank my mother, father and stepfather, who first gave me the opportunity to study at university, especially my mother, who always gave me strength and believed in my potential.

To all my friends who have been by my side throughout my journey.

I would like to thank my advisor, Prof. Dr. Manuela Corral, who was wonderful in all our discussions and helped me in the best possible way to complete the work successfully.

Finally, to all those who contributed directly or indirectly to the construction of this Course Conclusion.

SUMMARY

The aim of this work is to understand and analyze the new forms of sociability on the Internet, through a deeper understanding of cyberculture and cyberspace, and to identify the factors driving the growth not only of the digital market in Brazil and Belém, but also the ways in which companies have come to communicate with their customers. This work was based on theorists and thinkers from the digital scene. Research was also carried out into the advertising market in Belém, where three advertising agencies in the city were interviewed and analyzed in order to understand the current market situation and demand in the region.

Keywords: Cyberculture. Cyberspace. Digital market. Consumers.

INTRODUCTION

The internet is a worldwide phenomenon that is growing at a constant rate and has become an essential part of life and the way in which society interacts with each other, not only in personal relationships but also within the advertising market around the world. This work will discuss exactly this influence that the internet has on the lives of individuals, based on its growth and, above all, the emergence of technological means of communication that have created the opportunity for the internet to spread in such a way, becoming part of the lives of all its users, and especially those who are most dependent on the phenomenon.

Based on these considerations, this work aims to identify and analyze the new consumer profile and the way in which these individuals behave in the face of the expansive reach of the web within society, in order to better understand how cyberspace and cyberculture have been key processes for the growth and development of the digital market, especially in Brazil, where the percentage of online users and consumers is increasing every day, and also to analyze the way in which this new type of consumer has come to influence the growth of the advertising market in our country.

The digital market is expanding every day, mainly because of the large number of users of social networks and also because of the increased proximity of the relationship between company and customer, which has created a new way of interacting, where customers are more listened to and companies can position themselves in a more personal way with their public, In addition to the influence on companies, the new way of consuming and dealing with the recurring issues of everyday life has meant that not only these companies, but also small entrepreneurs and specific services such as communication agencies, have repositioned themselves and sought new horizons as a method of staying in the market.

The first chapter will look at the relationship between cyberculture and communication and the importance of the growth of cyberspace, in view of the ways in which individuals interact within platforms such as social networks, which currently have great power of influence and reach, especially for the use of *online* advertising.

The second chapter delves into the meaning of marketing, its definition and the emergence of marketing 3.0, based on the foundation of Philip Kotler (2010), which has become of paramount importance for the relationship and interaction of companies with their customers, where one can also perceive the growth of technologies and the change in the way individuals interact, based on the growth of the digital market in Brazil and Belém, related to the influence of the media and the need to recycle within the market.

In the third chapter we will understand the new forms of interaction between individuals in more depth, where their behavior and new profile come into question, identifying the factors that

name, "cyber" which is a diminutive of cybernetics, the science focused on advanced technology, and culture, which is part of humanity's identity, differentiating itself in each social group. And the combination of these two makes cyberculture encompass a virtual, technological and cultural world that has been developing over time.

> Cyberculture is the relationship between communication and information technologies and culture, which emerged from the convergence of computerization and telecommunication in the 1970s. It is a new relationship between technologies and sociability, shaping contemporary culture (LEMOS, cited by BASSO and DIEL, 2007).

André Lemos, a scholar in the field of communication, believes that cyberculture became part of society's culture from the 1970s onwards, because it was at this time that the first computers were created and human beings began to have a more personal relationship with these devices, and as a result of their improvements, they had the opportunity to expand their knowledge, and this was mainly due to the advent of the internet, which made it possible for internet users to be connected and communicate with each other more easily.

It can be said that cyberculture is a new social segment, where the human and technological relationship increases over time, and in a gigantic way, making the community increasingly dependent on the cyber and technological environment, in search of innovations and products that facilitate their efforts, whether at work or in their personal lives, with the creation of new computers, this search for technological improvements has only increased and tends to increase even more.

The ease of communicating via broadband has sparked a certain instinct for virtual necessity in all users of the net. It's common to see people with cell phones, tablets and even microcomputers everywhere, instant communication makes life easier for users and makes the internet increasingly present in society's daily life. And it was in the 1990s that the internet became part of people's lives in a more general way. In the past, access was much more restricted than it is today.

According to a survey by the Brazilian Telecommunications Association (Telebrasil), there were more than 130 million broadband accesses, mainly due to the 3g and 4g mobile internet networks, which accounted for half of all connections. This is the reality in Brazil, but we should also consider other countries, even so, the numbers only tend to grow, according to some teachers and students, the computer has become more present in carrying out activities in class, according to research from ICT Education 2013, carried out by the Internet Steering Committee in Brazil (CGI.br) through the Regional Center for Studies for the Development of the Information Society (CETIC.br), of the Ponto BR Information and Coordination Center (NIC.br).

Society's relationship with the Internet is getting closer and closer because, in addition to being an important means of communication as a conduit for fast information, the network also serves as a means of interaction between individuals, where communicating is getting easier and faster, everything is less complex and more practical, it's the great reality of the connected, information spreads in a matter of seconds from one side of the world to the other, and can reach from Brazil to China, all in the blink of an eye, or rather, in just one click. And one factor that contributes greatly to all this interaction is social networks, which connect thousands of people from all over the world on a single site.

Bringing together technology and society, cyberculture is a contemporary culture which is of paramount importance for interaction and communication, and is part not of everyday life, but of society itself, and has gradually infiltrated human culture until it is part of all, and can even be recognized as a "world culture", which is present in every social group in the community and which suffers influences and changes according to who uses it, but which is nevertheless present and important for everyone.

It is possible to be closer even at a distance, not just in personal relationships, but also in the relationship between companies and consumers, who have been increasing their *Social Medial* services in an attempt to create a more affective relationship with the customer, giving the feeling of closeness and companionship that we seek when we receive a call, be it for mere information or for complaints about the brand's products.

In "The Internet Galaxy", Castells believes that "The Internet is a new communication environment. Since communication is the essence of human activity, all domains of social life are being modified by the widespread uses of the Internet." (CASTELLS, 2003. p. 225). As a result, we can see that human beings have had communication as a necessity since the dawn of our existence, increasing the ease of communication with the use of the Internet and especially the mobile Internet, which provides the opportunity for one individual to connect with another, making it possible to interact from different locations.

According to the IBGE (http://www.ibge.gov.br/home) (Brazilian Institute of Geography and Statistics), more than half of Brazilians already have access to the internet. Data released in September 2014 shows that the number of internet users rose from 49.2% in 2012 to 50.1% in 2013, This information is part of the National Household Sample Survey (Pnad) for 2013. There were around 2.5 million internet users (2.9%) between 2012 and 2013, in other words, almost 86.7 million internet users aged 10 or over, not to mention the significant increase in the use of smartphones.

Graph 01: Internet Use by Region.

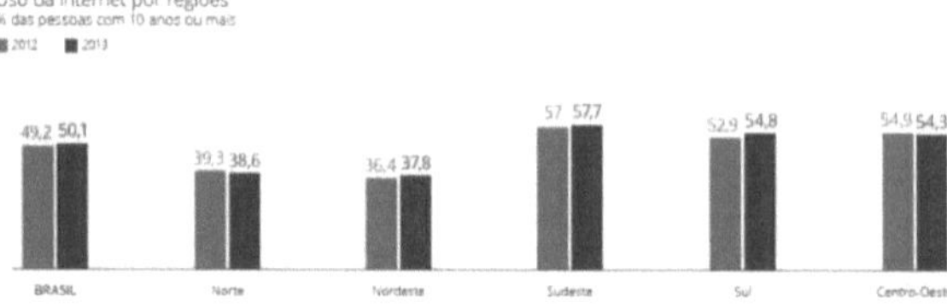

Source: Amanda Polato (Available at: http://tinyurl.com/lfws8f3).

In 2013, according to IDC (http://br.idclatin.com/), in the second quarter of the year there were more than 8.3 million smartphones sold in Brazil, or , an increase of 110% compared to the same period in 2012, and in 2014 it was no different, the number of sales increasing by 120% compared to 2013.

Ordinary cell phones have been replaced, giving way to smartphones and it doesn't stop there, Abinee (http://www.abinee.org.br/) (Electrical and Electronics Industry Association) projects an increase of 61%, half that recorded in 2013. And now it's not just teenagers who are connected, on the contrary, data from the National Household Sample Survey (PNAD) released in 2013 by the Brazilian Institute of Geography and Statistics (IBGE) also shows that the proportion of users has risen from 20.9% to 46.5% and as resistant as they are, Brazilians aged 50 and over are part of a large percentage of new internet users, with an increase from 7.3% to 18.4% of the population in this age group.

Graph 02: Cell Phone Use by Country Region.

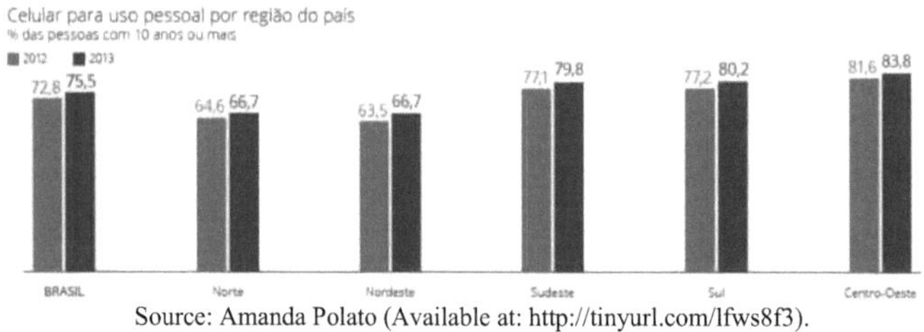

Source: Amanda Polato (Available at: http://tinyurl.com/lfws8f3).

The evolution of cyberculture has changed the way individuals act with each other and with technology itself, propagating a collective feeling in which the individual who is part of or connected to the network in some way, has the need to create, publish or propagate content, because this way, interaction takes place and information can reach other users of this means of communication, where everything can and everything is done and the more popularity it achieves the better. And along with this, technological changes also have their importance, because it is through their products that individuals remain connected to cyberspace.

Still in line with Castells' (2003) thinking, the great advance of the internet has taken place since its emergence to the present day. We live in a completely connected generation, be it X, Y or Z, everyone is involved in this great cyber revolution, everyone wants to see and be seen and this is one of the great factors that has kept social networks such as *Facebook*[2] and *Instagram*[3] popular, which enable the instant exchange of information such as images and videos. Everything is recorded and shared.

1.1. ONLINE MEDIA

It's impossible to talk about cyberculture and not relate it to the media, because since the internet emerged, various segments have been created from it, all strategically designed to be used in order to attract internet users into the cyber world, and online media is currently a major segment of the Brazilian advertising market. With a strong presence in the market, this department only tends to grow within the advertising environment, and we can easily see this with the increase in purchases and services made over the internet.

As we know, the mobility that the Internet gives us only increases its popularity among the public. After all, it's much more practical to make a payment online than to go to the bank and wait in a queue for who knows how long. And that's what the media sell, convenience, guaranteeing the minimum effort that the customer may have to make. The ease with which advertisements are published on the networks makes consumers look for information online, whether it's about prices or product quality.

Online media are of paramount importance for the execution of online advertising, as they are increasingly the target of advertisements and brand announcements, because it is due to the ease and lifespan of the advertisement that online media have a wide reach, creating even more focus for the network. The 21st century is undergoing a major revolution and the biggest contributing factor to this is the Internet and the consequences it brings to the lives of consumers and companies.

We know that many well-known brands such as Sky, Ponto Frio and Netshoes take advantage of the facilities provided by the internet to be closer to their customers. After all, everyone likes to be seen, and feeling important is essential, especially in the relationship between customer and company. And the power that this relationship of companionship has to attract the affinity of the public is one of the great strengths of large and small companies, which seek to be

---

[1] Social Media: Services used by companies in online media.
[2] Facebook: Website and social networking service that was launched on February 4, 2004, operated and privately owned by Facebook Inc.
[3] Instagram: Online photo and video sharing social network that allows users to take photos and videos.

ever closer to their target audience.

1.1.2. The power of the media

Along with the internet, the media has revolutionized the market, because with its help it is possible for internet users/consumers to keep abreast of the current situation in the market and the world in general, and this is of paramount importance for companies, because consumers want to know about what they are buying, in other words, if your company is not easily found in a search on the net, you lose the opportunity to do business. It has become natural to publish advertising content in the media and as this content comes in large quantities, it is necessary to readjust so that your product/company is better and better.

> It has become commonplace to say that the new information and communication technologies are changing not only the forms of entertainment and leisure, but potentially all spheres of society (ROBINS and WEBSTER 1999, p. 111).

Based on Warner Robins and Merriam Webster's assertion, it can be understood that even before the full reach of the Internet, information and communication technologies were already integrally linked to everything that human beings are connected to; in other words, we can relate past and future. Until a while ago, it wasn't imagined that the computer would stop being just a diversion, with games and a few image and video programs, and would become socially important in Brazilians' lifestyles. This importance is easy to see in everyday life, especially with the increase in the use of broadband networks in the country and how the number of Internet users continues to rise.

And that's why big companies are investing more and more in online advertising, because taking into account the data on growth in too much in Brazil, this is the advertising market's big chance, so that there's more interaction with the public and thus reach more and more people and get a satisfactory result. The media is very important in communication precisely because it's immediate, practical and fast, where the content can have a longer lifespan than it would in a magazine, for example, and thus reach a larger audience.

According to data from E-bit (http://www.animamidia.com.br/tag/ebit/), 51.3 million people have already used the internet at least once to buy a product, and the increase in mobile internet use was the factor that helped consumers make purchases online, not to mention that approximately 9 million Brazilians are expected to make their first purchase online, increasing the number of virtual consumers to 60 million.

IAB Brasil (http://iabbrasil.net/portal/) (Interactive Advertising Bureau) points out that online media is the type of advertising that Brazilians consider most important, 40% of those interviewed spend at least two hours connected, while 27% spend the same amount of time watching TV, and the products most used for access are Tablets and Smartphones. Not to mention that the majority of these individuals spent around 14 hours using the services of these devices to connect to the internet within a week, also using the service to watch TV.

> Contemporary technology has become an increasingly everyday force, integrating itself into the lives of millions and millions of people all over the world, from the workplace to the domestic sphere, from places of leisure to the fields of war (RUDIGER, 2007. p. 67).

As seen in the quote above, Rudiger sees cyberculture as a contemporary technology with great strength, and this can be explained by the need to stay connected and also by the way in which the market is growing dramatically in this medium. Media such as *Facebook has* over 65 million users in Brazil, and 41.2 million users on *Twitter*[4] , after the USA, Brazil is *YouTube's* biggest market[5] . However, the media is not just about social networks like these, it also includes blogs, websites and portals. All ready to attract audiences and expand their reach, thus expanding the advertising submitted to each of them.

And from 2013 to 2017, Brazil is set to be the fastest-growing online media market, with 18% of advertising on the internet, while the rest of the world will only have around 13%. The numbers are only increasing, as is Brazilians' access to the internet, making it possible for advertising on the web to be more widespread, not to mention the increase in demand from the advertising market outside the internet as well, because with this growth, agencies will have the opportunity to improve their services more and more and invest in digital marketing to meet the demands of the market.

[4] Twitter: Social network and microblogging server that allows users to send and receive personal updates from other contacts.
[5] Youtube: Website that allows its users to upload and share videos in digital format.

Graph 03: Projected Annual Growth (PWC)

Growth by segment -% compound average annual growth projected 2013 ~ 2017

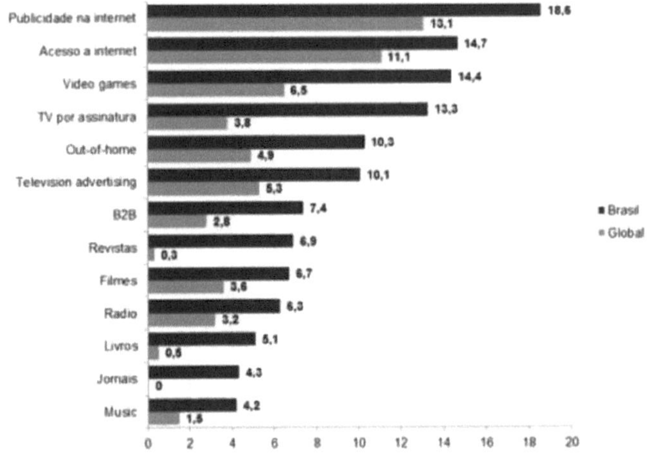

Source: Projegoes PWC (Available at: http://tinyurl.com/owsxs46)

It is for this reason that advertising attention is focused on Brazil, where the growth of this type of media is increasingly noticeable, both in terms of the increase in the use of electronic devices with Internet access and the access to the network itself, where more and more Brazilians have the opportunity to be connected. The data is there to prove that communication is essential for the evolution of society. We need to stay connected and, above all, constantly recycle ourselves so that our ideas remain valid and make sense; in a world that is constantly changing due to the speed and lifespan of subjects/information, being "in the know" is essential.

An important segment of the media is the social networks, which use the most advertising, ranging from ads created by the pages themselves to advertising created by the users themselves, which is reflected a lot in services, especially in the case of small businesses. Not to mention the fact that the Internet induces users to make more online purchases due to the large number of advertisements on websites and social networks, because these consumers say that the Internet helps them gather information about a particular product, something that media such as TV and magazines don't do.

Society has undergone several changes in the course of our evolution and one of these has been the cybernetic revolution, which covers more space every second, creating great dependence for its users. And in the course of its evolution, the web has influenced the way individuals relate to each other.

1.1.3. Social networks

Much of the advertising on the Internet is done through social networks, which generally use online banners to advertise brands and products. The most common is on social networks like *Facebook,* which has a large number of users. In Brazil alone, there are 76 million active users. What's even more interesting is that most of them connect via mobile devices such as cell phones and tablets. And according to Alexandre Hohagem, Vice President of *Facebook* in Latin America, "These numbers have great marketing power." And companies are already aware that this type of advertising is the big *boom* in the market.

> In order to go beyond individual attributes and consider the relationships between social actors, social network analysis seeks to focus on new "units of analysis", such as: relationships (characterized by content, direction and strength), social lakes (which connect pairs of actors through one or more relationships), multiplexity (the more relationships a social lake has, the greater its multiplexity) and the composition of the social lake (derived from the individual attributes of the actors involved). (RECUERO, 2009. p. 3).

From the point of view of Raquel Recuero, a cyberculture scholar, we can understand social networks as a means of individual interaction, even though it is a collective communication, each individual searches for what interests them, and the more they identify with the content, the broader it becomes, In this case, Recuero believes that these attitudes are changing the way in which blogs, *Facebook, Twitter* and other means of interacting on the Internet act, in a way, including interests and individuals in a single means of interaction, thus achieving their ideal, which is to be popular.

Following this line of thought, it can be said that social networks are changing the meaning of the relationships built on the internet and the way in which this has repercussions on society's social and informational processes. In other words, the internet has an influence both on and off the net, because the way in which individuals interact with each other has been changing over time, and this doesn't just apply to cyberspace, but to "real" society. The way in which this reflects on the social and cultural aspects of society is what makes Recuero believe that social networks are governed by a body of actors, who act as molders of social structures through interaction and the constitution of social lakes.

Even so, Recuero sees the networks as an individualistic object, in the sense that each of its users can take on different roles within the network, where they can represent multiple faces of their identity, and this can easily be seen in the need that people have to show things via social networking sites, whether it's a photo, a video or sharing a *status*[6] , the important thing is that there is something to be shared, so that people can see it and, in a way, the individual shows what they

[6] Status: Within social networks, a status is a sentence or text in which a person describes their situation.

are or what they are not but would like to be.

"An individual can be understood not only through the groups (networks) to which he belongs, but also through the positions he holds within these networks." (WATTS 2003 cited by RECUERO 2009, p. 3). Based on Watts' idea, the interactivity of social networks is due precisely to the fact that individuals, despite their inequalities, often have similar social and ideological views, which means that this interaction only increases, because with each shared publication millions of users are reached, thus creating greater scope for this interaction.

Initially, some sociologists believed in social networks as dyads (relationships between two people would be the smallest relational structure in society), in other words, the relationship between individuals would occur in a random way, which would affect everyone, indeterminately. This can be related to the sharing of certain things that end up reaching all kinds of people, who would have no relation to each other. And the second focus of analysis would be triads (two people with a friend in common), so the view of triads is that these two people who don't know each other but have a friend in common are more inclined to receive information passed on by them than information from another individual who is not in their same cycle, and this information passed on from friends in common is more likely to be within the interests of this individual than of one who is not part of the same cycle.

We can thus understand that this relationship is relative, because when we are connected we are prone to receiving any type of information, we just need to be aware of what we will consider productive or not, the main fact is that we live in a completely digital age where everything we do is seen and commented on and contemporary technology has made this attitude normal, because this is how we will have more popularity within social networks and even outside them, today's world needs this type of interaction both personally and professionally.

And the number of users on social networks is only increasing, and the most popular among them are social networking sites, a great example of which is *Facebook,* which in Brazil alone has reached more than 65 million users, not to mention *Twitter,* which is also a very popular social network in Brazil and is an example of interactivity between consumers and companies.

The great importance of the Internet's popularity is the fact that it helps the advertising market, which expands in step with its users, who connect and are always on the lookout for new things, making this medium the big "apple of the eye" of the Brazilian and even international market, which, based on research into the popularity of Internet advertising in Brazil, ends up attracting not only brands and companies from within the country but also from abroad, and in the following chapter we will show how this growth is taking place in the advertising market in Brazil and Belém.

2. DIGITAL MARKETING

2.1. DEFINITION OF MARKETING

Before tackling the subject at a national level, let's first define its concept. Although broad, marketing is defined as a set of techniques and methods aimed at sales concepts. More than just an advertising method, marketing has a social meaning, which can influence and attract the public so that they get what they want by creating, offering and exchanging products. The word marketing derives from *Market,* which in English means market. In other words, marketing goes beyond selling products, you need to know how and what to do to get the public interested in what you are selling.

The process goes from the creation and planning of the product to its arrival at the consumer, so marketing is seen as a key process for companies, mainly because it covers not only the product area but also the company itself, where it is possible to define the way in which they will interact and behave towards the market and their customers, as well as internally, because before becoming great within the market, you need to be great within your own establishment, strengthening the relationships of your workers and customers.

And with the potential growth of the internet and the increase in the number of users on social networks, marketing has gained new forms of interaction, because, in addition to knowing how to work in a media that reaches the most diverse types of audiences, it is necessary to take measures so that this work becomes productive and even massive, because, in this way, it is possible for digital marketing to reach a greater number of users.

The so-called 3.0 marketing began to be used and practiced after the great revolution we experienced with the internet, which meant that companies and customers could have a closer relationship, thereby attracting more customers and retaining those who were already loyal to a particular company, and thus also completely influencing the way in which marketing is carried out on the digital stage.

2.1.2. Marketing 3.0.

Philip Kotler (2010) believes that starting to use marketing 3.0 within companies is essential for success in the digital market, which, because it is growing and has more vision, is nowadays one of the greatest ways of reaching the public, whatever it may be, because the vast majority are part of cyberspace and this number is only increasing, so the great idea of marketing 3.0 is that by listening to customers it is possible to know what needs to be done to satisfy their needs, creating their aspirations, while at the same time helping the world, because showing concern for both the public and the planet itself is paramount to increasing the bond created between company and customer.

Following the pace of interaction between web users themselves, marketing 3.0 is the great interest of digital marketing for companies, because it is from this that the ways of communicating with the public become increasingly easier and more efficient, after all, the consumer profile has changed as a result of the ways in which the internet has made it possible for individuals to interact with each other, and the advertising market has had to shape itself so that this new consumer attitude becomes something positive for its numbers and market demands, and this is what can be observed in Kotler's work, which will be better understood in the following chapter, which will analyze the forms of behavior of these new consumers.

The mission of this marketing is to present new ideals, and this is done by getting closer to the public, because from this approach it is possible to know what causes the most commotion or reactions, be they positive or even negative, which sometimes have a positive effect for the company, although this is difficult, but many are known from internet publications and whether they like it or not, this ends up being important for their popularity. You need to know what actions will be taken, what approaches will be taken with consumers and what will be done to make consumers more aware of the company and thus become interested in the products and services on offer.

Figure 01: Basic elements of MKT 3.0

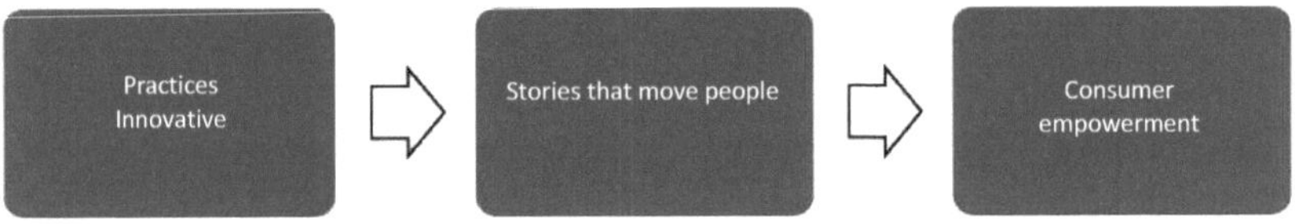

Practices Innovative	⇨	Stories that move people	⇨	Consumer empowerment

Source: (Produced by the author, 2014)

The image above shows three important steps in the implementation of marketing 3.According to Kotler (2010), the main focus is on making the company create a certain link with the customer, and this will be done by creating stories that excite, as we can see in various television commercials, the great emotional appeal that current advertisements have on the consumer and this serves to spread the work of the company, because it is from innovative practices that handles will be created that will emote and attract more attention from the consumer, consequently influencing the decision-making power that each one has, because society is easily moved and tends to swing more towards the emotional side, because this involves memories or various factors and feelings acquired over the course of the life of each of these individuals.

It is from the execution of the marketing plan that the company developers' idea will be disseminated, and this idea will only be successful if it is embraced by the *mainstream* market[7] so that it has the desired impact, in other words, so that it has consumer participation, whether in the form of shares, comments or likes, the more consumers who have access to what the company is broadcasting, the better, because, as has already been said, this influences the *empowerment*[8] of the public, which is their ability to choose and decide in relation to the product or the company, in this case.

"As consumers become more collaborative, cultural and spiritual, the character of marketing also changes." (KOTLER, 2010, p.23). With this phrase, Kotler defines well the way in which consumers are interacting in the *online* market, and many companies are taking advantage of this new way of acting to consolidate themselves within the market, increasing their presence within social networks, for example, which is where there is considerable media growth, especially in Brazil.

As you can see, through marketing, the ways in which companies will deal and act both internally and externally are planned to the millimeter, because it is with this planning that a company will establish itself in the market, and it is from this that its target audience will be defined and the areas and ways in which interactions with the consumer will be carried out.

The way in which the company acts with the consumer is a factor of the utmost importance, because it is from this relationship that the company will make the customer feel secure and increasingly willing and inclined to receive information and proposals for products or actions linked to this company, so the more special and close to the company the customer feels, because one of the needs of the new consumer is to feel important, and with the help of marketing strategies this feeling is possible, and companies are increasingly increasing their participation in the online advertising scene in Brazil.

This scenario has increased and continues to increase with the passage of time and with the changes in technologies and means of communication that have arisen from the demands of the public, which means that products are increasingly improved and advanced.

2.2. THE GROWTH OF TECHNOLOGIES AND FORMS OF INTERACTION IN SOCIETY WITHIN CYBERSPACE

[7] Mainstream: Main current, in the sense of the trend of a given historical period of an activity.
[8] Empowerment: This is based on delegating decision-making powers to the consumer.

It was in 1945 that the first computers came into existence, actually better known as programmable calculators that made it possible to store programs. Previously only used by the military for scientific calculations, it was around the 1960s that civilian use became widespread, clearly already showing signs of the great growth of both machines and the performance and capacity of their equipment and reach before humanity. According to Rudiger (2007), technology is becoming increasingly powerful and present in society and in all places, be they workplaces or personal.

The first commercial computer was the LEO, produced in 1954 by the J. Lyons company with the aim of speeding up the work in its offices. Other machines continued to be manufactured, such as the UNIVAC (Universal Automatic Computer) model, which was improved to receive instructions from a magnetic tape instead of using perforated cards, which made the work more efficient. The UNIVAC was also used during a presidential election to predict the outcome of votes. From then on, the process continued and the machines became more and more evolved, with more functions until the development of the personal computer, capable of storing data such as images, texts and music, left aside its exclusive "participation" of companies and gave way to a new technological process.

As time went by, the computer gained more space in society, becoming part of human life as a whole, in this case, being present in their workplaces and homes, also giving space for more innovations and improvements, which would become indispensable, generating a certain addiction to use and the need to obtain better and more advanced machines. And in the 80s of the 20th century, this could be clearly seen: the computer became part of a new horizon, even more improved, making room for multimedia, ceasing to be a product of technical exclusivity, and joining telecommunication, cinema, publishing and television. It is very useful for communication and interactivity, with games and the possibility of working with interactive messages.

In his work "Cyberculture, Pierre Levy (1999)" discusses the emergence of cyberspace and cyberculture, treating them as a strong means of interaction for society, and from that moment he already foresaw the great popularization of information technologies and the growth of cyberspace, also foreseeing the possible socio-cultural changes that it would have over time and the influence that the network would have on the most diverse segments. Also noting the importance of this means of communication for today's society, and based on this, it can be said that the digital market is a key segment in the growth of Internet advertising and the potential of the Brazilian market.

2.3. DIGITAL MARKET IN BRAZIL

According to the IAB Brasil (Interactive Advertising Bureau) (http://iabbrasil.net/), the country is considered a world power in the digital arena, which is due to the considerable increase in Internet users, and ends up generating greater investment for Brazil's digital segment. And it doesn't stop there, because every day this number of users increases, leading companies large and small to be forced to fit in with the great online demand and make this means of communication one of the most important ways of interacting and being closer to their consumers, who are increasingly demanding and aware of the changes that are taking place in the way they are and should be treated.

Taking advantage of this new way of consumer interaction, many of these companies have been changing and molding themselves to be able to meet the demands, not to mention the increase in *online* media, because it is through ease that the customer is attracted, after all, this is one of the main roles of the Internet, to bring facilities, be they in communication between individuals or in the way of finding information of various kinds. And along with the media, the growth of online shopping has also increased, which generates profit both for specific sites for this type of service and for the companies that make these products available online.

According to a study of the number of investments in media by IAB Brasil (http://tinyurl.com/qhgkmje), with the help of portals and advertisers, the internet is an important market for Brazilian commerce and is on the rise, gaining more and more users, causing more and more companies to look for digital services in order to be included and participate in this positive process that the digital market is going through. As a result, digital agencies are gaining more and more space, because with the specialization of their work, the number of clients is only increasing, as the market is new and not all companies have specific areas for this type of service, i.e. the greater the number of users, the greater the increase in investment in *e-commerce*[9] in Brazil.

It is based on the increase in users of social networks such as *Facebook* that marketing plans are applied, because, in Kotler's view, this is how companies will reach the consumer, and through social networks the company's approach is easier, because the speed and expansion of the content generated in this segment is greater than in other places on the web such as corporate sites.

The *e-commerce* market has seen considerable growth in the online sales sector, and according to E-Bit (http://www.ebit.com.br/) the estimated increase in the *e-commerce* sector is 15% in the second half of 2014, and could reach a turnover of R$35 billion reais. Compared to 2013, the percentage increase is 25%, meaning that there are around 104 million e-commerce orders. Even so, the sector that leads online sales is fashion and accessories, which accounts for 18% of sales, ahead of categories such as cosmetics and perfumery (16%) and household appliances (11%).

Gaining 5.06 million consumers in the first half of 2014 alone, or 27% more than in the first half of 2013, the *e-commerce* sector is only getting stronger, with ever-increasing and more

[9] E-commerce: Commercial buying and selling operations carried out on the Internet.

interesting numbers in the eyes of the Brazilian market, It is on the basis of these results that investments are increasing and this segment is recognized in Brazil, and by generating more investment, it consequently generates more demand, because the greater the number of advertisements on the web, the greater the demand from consumers reached by this category, and social networks are segments with great value for this type of advertising.

The largest numbers of *online* purchases are made via mobile devices, and the profit of R$560 million in 2013 increased to R$1.13 billion, an average of 102% compared to the same period the previous year. In 2014 alone, the number of orders reached 2.890 million, and the main devices used in these purchases are tablets (60%) and smartphones (40%), all through the use of applications made available for cell phones and tablets. Women lead the fashion sector, also known as *m-consumers,* with 57%, while men account for the remaining 43%, and classes A and B account for 64% of consumers and classes C and D account for 25%, with the remainder (11%) choosing not to state their income.

With this data we can once again see the real growth that the *online* media market has been achieving in Brazil over the years. User numbers that used to be very low due to the lack of inclusion of individuals on the Internet, today are developing an extraordinary change that is not only interesting for showing the country's development index in terms of the inclusion of citizens in one of society's communication segments, but also shows how the advertising market is growing considerably in Brazil, where, despite narrowing the market, it is necessary for it to grow, influencing the growth of a new media segment, which receives a lot of expectations from the market, as it grows and increases the country's economic potential.

This market is growing mainly due to the fact that advertising, like consumers, has changed over time and also with the socio-cultural changes in Brazil, where advertising has new interactions, new ways of reaching the public, also taking into account the new forms of entertainment and means of interaction in society, means such as social networks and applications such as *Whatsapp*[10 11] or *Viber*[1] . for example.

2.3.1. Media and Business in the Digital Landscape

A 2010 survey by Deloitte (a brand that brings together various professionals from firms around the world to provide services such as auditing, consultancy and the like) focused on media within companies and how and which services are most used by these companies when entering the online market, it can be understood that the media have opened up a new way for a company to be

[10] Whatsapp: Instant messaging program for smartphones.
[11] Viber: Application that allows you to make free calls to other cell phones or computers that also have it installed.

more present in the market, in this case, companies use the media as a form of leverage to increase their popularity among the public, thus showing how companies can benefit by creating strategies to get closer to their customers.

The study carried out by Deloitte also shows that social media are used more as a means of advertising than as a relationship platform, once again reaffirming the increase and value that the growth of *e-commerce* consumers has for the market, as well as indicating what kind of attitude companies should take to attract these consumers.

type of consumer, and ways of identifying them in order to know what to do and how to plan strategies to increase online demand for a particular company's products. And that's when we come back to Kotler's marketing 3.0 thinking, where a company must improve its behavior, as well as its marketing strategies in order to persuade consumers, making them receptive to the product offers coming from the company, where he [the consumer] will have the power to decide what he likes best.

In the graph below, we can see which tools companies use most on social media, so we can see that their main focus is on marketing campaigns, which are designed to publicize products and services that attract the public and make the company profit. The graph also shows that brand or market monitoring is widely used, mainly because of the need to be aware of how the company is being perceived or how market sectors are doing, thus giving large and small companies the opportunity to identify with greater credibility what is lacking, what is pleasing and what is best for the relationship with their online customers.

Graph 04: Percentage of Most Exploited Media Apps in Companies.

Marketing accounts for 83% of social media initiatives

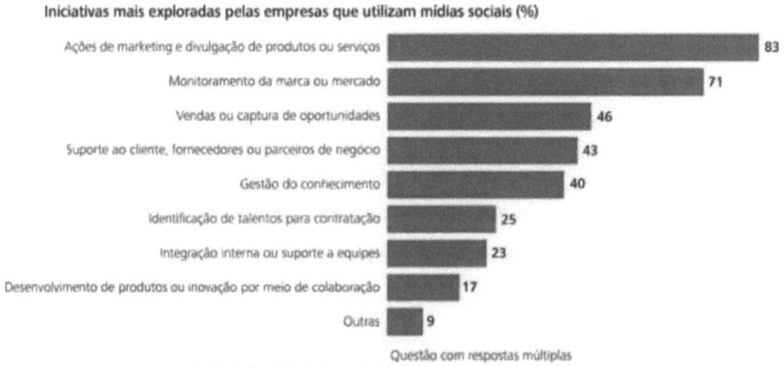

Source: Deloitte 2010 (Available at: http://www.deloitte.com/).

Another major factor responsible for the popularity of companies on social networks is the famous word-of-mouth, which comes from the process of information being passed from one user to another, because, according to Raquel Recuero (2009), we understand that despite being unified, the internet is individualistic in the sense that each user will give their opinion and spread what is of interest to them, but from the moment a user publishes a certain subject, this subject reaches a large part of the users of the network, because what is shared passes through friends of friends and so on.

The main enemy for companies may be the lack of time to carry out social media monitoring and management activities. According to data from Deloitte, 49% of companies say that these are their main challenges, and this is also due to a lack of investment, It can be seen that despite being aware that the digital market is a sector that is growing more and more every day and that both today and in the future it will continue to be very important for the solidification of companies in the segment, investments are also increasing, and with this the chances of these companies being more "connected" to the online consumer are also increasing, which will provide more recognition for the companies.

The problem of media management failure is a reality for some companies in Brazil, which have not yet adapted to what the market is demanding lately, and because of this, the need to readjust and be fit for the demands of the market, some companies hire specialized media services, consequently increasing the insertion of digital agencies in the country.

2.3.2. The Work of Digital Agencies

It was based on the needs of the market that the first communication agencies began to be created, specializing their services exclusively for *online* media. Inspired by the growth of the digital scene in Brazil, digital agencies have a number of different segments, among them, there are agencies that are more focused on technology, agencies that specialize in campaign creation and media management, and agencies that basically bring together all of the above, in other words, a complete and more specific agency for working with large companies, for example.

Agencies focused on technology specialize in application systems and have vast knowledge in developing solutions, while those that specialize in campaign creation and media management develop digital communication, with an efficient plan for public relations agencies and campaigns, in each of which the planning and management is in the hands of the company. The third agency, which would be the most complete of all, works with web management consultancy, i.e. this type of agency involves numerous segments, ranging from technology to building websites, virtual stores and even planning online campaigns, working mainly with the company as a whole.

It is the digital agency or department that will define the best strategy for the agencies to be implemented by the companies, presenting them to the company's specialized sector, which will give the final word based on the *know-how*[12] of the agency's consulting area. In order to know what type of agency to hire, first of all the company needs to define which sectors it wants digital agencies to work in, and it is from there that the company is able to define the type of service that will be used to improve its services.

Paulo Kendzerski is CEO of WBI Brasil, vice-president of Federasul, and believes that it is necessary to think carefully when choosing the digital agency that will serve your company, because results happen if everyone works in harmony and complements each other's specialties. By this, Kendzerski meant that the relationship between the two sectors, the agency and the company, needs to be in tune for the work to achieve the expected success, and this is only possible if both work together, determining exactly what should be done by each party.

According to the Brazilian Association of Digital Agencies (http://www.abradi.com.br/) (ABRADI), there are 93 digital agencies associated with its website, which provides information on each of these agencies and also information on the market and on the association itself, why it exists and the importance of this is that we can get to know some of the existing agencies in Brazil and also observe how the market has been acting and how these agencies behave in the face of cyber changes in the advertising market.

As we can see, the digital market in Brazil is a segment with strong growth potential, given that the figures and percentages are there to prove that we have evolved in the advertising sector and will continue to evolve, just like the rest of the country, the digital market in Belém also needs to renew itself and invest even more in media, not only agencies but also large and small companies in the region, because the online sector is something that cannot go unnoticed in the eyes of the market, on the contrary, it is essential that it be explored more and more.

2.3.3. Digital Market in Belém

Over time, the growth of cyberculture and the need to keep up with the rest of the world has meant that technology has run alongside this phenomenon, forcing the market - not just technology, but the whole of it - to become an indispensable part of every individual's life, so that it can keep up with the changing needs of those it connects with and so, with each change, realign itself until it is once again within the standards imposed by the public, which is becoming more demanding as time goes by and the options for supplying its products increase. Thus, the service provider either meets this demand or it may not be suitable for the market and will need to review its concepts as a company/agency.

[12] Know-how: A term used to describe practical knowledge of how to do something.

With this in mind, the study of the Belém advertising market began, seeking to understand how agencies position themselves in the face of market changes, based on what the client wants and the image that the agency conveys to its public.

The Professional Association of Advertising Agencies of the State of Pará (http://www.sinapropa.com.br/site/2014/) (SINAPRO-PA) was founded in 1983, and has 33 member agencies, which are not exclusively in the digital sector. In a survey conducted among some of the state's agencies in order to understand their needs and the differences in the way they operate in the market, it was possible to analyze that the majority of them have a digital sector, while some have only recently been set up, others have already been created especially to serve this segment.

In an interview conducted on the occasion of this work, with advertising executive Philippe Medeiros, Marketing Analyst in Digital Platforms at CA Comunicagao, we discussed the subject of the digital market in Pará and Medeiros believes that the digital market in Pará is still in its infancy, because, as well as being an innovation, the number of professionals in the area is still scarce, and when he talks about a small number, he's talking about people who are qualified for the market, and that although clients and agencies are aware of the importance of digital for their development in the market, the investment is not enough to please a sector that has much more to offer. Not to mention the large number of agencies called "Digital Agencies" or "Social Media" that undervalue the rest of the agencies by charging prices that are not up to the standard charged by larger, more complete agencies, which means that companies seek out this type of service because it is more "affordable" rather than investing in work that is actually qualified to meet the needs of the client/company.

Medeiros believes that clients still see the digital service as free or cheap, in which case it's very easy to hire an unqualified person to publish content on a social network, for example. However, these clients don't realize that the agency's service isn't just about generating content; on the contrary, there's much more to offer, such as *Social Media*[13] , *Display*[14] , *Search*[15] and others, which make up the vast world of digital. Therefore, clients/companies need to see that search engines, portals and social platforms deserve greater attention, attention that Philippe refers to as a strong means of generating profit, not only for the digital agency but also for the company that invests in media such as these.

Profits are made by targeting ads, which yields even better results than prime-time spots on

13 Social Media: Department that involves various activities integrated with technology, social interactions and the construction of words, videos, photos and music.

14 Display: Advertising term used for the visual presentation of information.

15 Search: The act of looking for specific content, either within the site itself or on all the servers available for searching.

TV stations such as Globo, because most internet users are more inclined to receive any kind of information, and when we talk about information, we mean ads that are strategically planned to reach certain and varied groups on the net, which makes it possible for the message to reach a wider audience.

The ideal thing would be to show companies in Pará that the type of campaign that currently has the greatest reach is hybrid advertising, which is defined as a new type of "advertising", and hybrid advertising is formed by the union of three media organizations: the advertising market, the entertainment industry and interactive technologies. In other words, relying more on the potential of digital, resorting to new means of communication and interaction with the consumer, because, with the use of this hybrid segment, the possibilities of the scenario only increase.

> Covaleski presents the reality of advertising that breaks away from the conventional, combining the functions of announcing, entertaining and interacting, "a new advertising communication for new senders and receivers", these hybrid solutions, so that "advertising communication then needs to establish a relationship not between brand and product, but between the brand and the content of interest to the consumer." (COVALESKI quoted by LAURINDO, 2012, p. 64).

With this in mind, it is understood that today's advertising market needs to break away from "outdated" methods, in this case thinking of new strategies to attract the public. After all, it is no coincidence that socio-cultural changes have given a certain force to society's relationship with the Internet, and it is from this type of change that new means of technological interaction have emerged, the increase in the use of devices that make it possible to use mobile internet, and also the way in which individuals have come to interact, not just with each other, but in response to the media developed on the web, in other words, changes that have occurred in the course of the evolution of society and the advertising market, which must see the new media as sources of rapprochement and profit generation.

Corporate communication needs to establish a greater bond with the consumer, not just to attract a larger audience to itself, but to think even more about its customers and plan ways of winning them over without it being necessary for the public to consume something, in this case, before selling to customers, generating ways of satisfying them or in this case, the way in which it deals with its customers and the market. The great thing about today's market is the consumer, not that it wasn't in the past, but looking for ways to win over the public is essential for the "new type of communication" between company and customer.

This "new type of communication" can be exemplified in the way in which the relationship between the two parties takes place, because the profile of the consumer has changed and companies need to adapt to please everyone, not to mention technological changes. It is these changes that have caused individuals' attitudes to change, to be molded along with the growth of means of communication such as the Internet, and this is what the digital market must observe, the way in which individuals act among themselves and within the network.

In Marketing 3.0, Kotler talks about different types of marketing, all focused on how companies can obtain a greater number of loyal customers, and at one point, Kotler talks about Collaborative Marketing, where the company will encourage the public to interact either through company posts, campaigns or even directly with the company through specific sites or sites such as "Reclame aqui", which is a site created especially for consumer complaints. We are living in the age of participation, where everyone wants to complain about their rights or express their ideas and thoughts about what the media is telling them. Consumers are more inclined to interact and it seems they like it.

3. CONSUMER BEHAVIOR

By studying the digital market at a national level and the way in which consumers react to the changes imposed by the updating of the means of communication and, above all, the distribution of information at this stage, we will be able to better understand this new form of interaction that companies and agencies have started to use in the face of this new type of consumer and, above all, understand the importance of this relationship for the growth of the digital market in Brazil.

We must understand that there are various types of consumers, and the combination of the roles of each of these consumers helps the way in which the public has been acting lately, in terms of consuming certain products or means of obtaining information or even making complaints and identifying possible improvements to the services of certain companies or products/services, This means that this new profile encompasses consumer profiles as a whole, as well as selecting where and what to buy, ranging from online stores with affordable prices to stores such as the famous Louis Vuitton brand, in other words, the individual has the opportunity to research what is more affordable, find out information about certain products, take advantage of the use of the internet as a whole, as a source of interaction and, above all, of information.

Just as man creates technological innovations that bring changes to the market, these innovations also change the way in which individuals interact. Since the emergence of new technologies, the way in which the public behaves has gradually changed in line with the evolution of the internet, which has also changed the way in which these individuals interact with each other, influencing the way in which information is passed on or even their interest in it.

We live in an age where everything is shared and more and more connected individuals are exposed, whether these messages are productive or not. Users of the web are subject to any and all messages that are published, whether from another state or even another country, The ease with which information circulates on the Internet means that information spreads in a matter of seconds, which is why some companies work so hard on this medium, because the public is more interested when the interest is visibly perceived on both sides, in this case, feeling important is paramount for this new type of consumer.

In the past, consumers had less practical options, where they had to go to a store, find out about products in the store itself or through customer service agents, who often stress more than they help, because customers like to feel important, as has already been said, and the customer's relationship with a telephone agent who generally has a somewhat robotic attitude ends up being negative for the company itself, But the fact is that new ways of finding out about and researching certain subjects have made everything more practical, because it's much more pleasant to make a purchase or pay a bill online than to have to spend time going to a store or bank and face an unpleasant queue. The changes to the web have given impetus to a new way of consuming, creating a new type of consumer, who is more present and increasingly seeking their rights as a customer.

3.1. THE NEW CONSUMER PROFILE

Kotler believes that marketing 3.0 is of the utmost importance for a company to establish itself in the market and, above all, by using this tool, to get closer to its customers, which will lead them to be more receptive to what is offered to them as a product. This attitude, which generates a closer relationship between the customer and the company, can be recognized as a trend in the forms of consumption and relationships in today's market, which is precisely due to the fact that we are living in a time of extreme exchange of information, where the main mediators and drivers are the users of the network.

Hebert Marshall McLuhan, a renowned Canadian philosopher and communication theorist, quoted a certain phrase, which says "Men create tools, tools recreate men", in observance of what Marshall McLuhan says in his phrase, it can be said that this is the current relationship of society in relation to the great inventions and technological changes that we have gone through and continue to go through, the experience of a generation extremely linked to the interactivity of the virtual world. In other words, society has undergone changes as well as new inventions, both in terms of products and even the internet, which is changing and reaching more and more users, and it is the internet, technology and the need for human beings to reinvent themselves that have led to these behavioral changes.

Everyone is connected and all the time, the reality is that we are living in a kind of new reality, you could say, where the individual is in one place but can be in several others through mobile devices connected to the Internet, which allow individuals to interact with each other and with the world, having access to information from the most varied places and communicating instantly, where everything is easier and more practical to do, without any effort, just with the help of sending a simple message or posting on social networks, for example, posts that are just as wide-ranging as offline media, which, by the way, are losing some of their space to the online structure, and the personal way in which this type of media is proposed to the public.

> The generational struggles over what is necessary and desirable show another way of establishing identities and building our difference. We are moving away from the era in which identities were defined by a-historical essences: today they are shaped by consumption, they depend on what you have, or what you can get hold of. (CANCLINI, quoted by VIEIRA, 2011, p. 3)

According to Nestor Garcia Canclini (1999), an Argentine anthropologist, consumers are facing a real struggle, more mental than otherwise, because the construction of the identity of individuals who lived without the Internet and have started to integrate it into their lives is different from that of people who were born into this era and also different from those who, despite using the medium, still remain withdrawn from its voluptuous world, In other words, individuals are increasingly constructing their identities through the influences caused by the internet, or rather, the way in which information reaches them. In this case, creating yourself in the virtual world is a major challenge for each individual, because it's through your profile that you will be in society or not, and this can easily be seen in the need to be seen and to be in evidence on the net.

It's true that consumers already existed before the internet, but what we're seeing is that this need to consume has become stronger as a result of the growth, not only of the evolution of the internet but also with the increase in the number of users connected to cyberspace, in other words, more and more people are influenced to consume what the media shows. So, as Canclini says, the identity of these individuals is based more on what they have or what they can consume, reinforcing the idea that the consumer profile is getting stronger and stronger and that companies are benefiting more and more from this.

We can perceive these identities not only through the demand for consumption on the web, but also by observing the attitudes of those connected, which vary in the most diverse ways depending on the subject, causing a publication to generate countless reactions and emotions.

Based on what is published, each individual decides whether it is of interest to them or not, and with the passage of time and the changes in coexistence that those connected to cyberspace have undergone, it has been possible to observe that although they are different individuals with different thoughts and beliefs, each one is interconnected with the other, in a way, increasing the circle of information propagated and, above all, the way in which this information is received, of course, in different ways according to each profile on the network, and this is precisely because we improve this means of communication according to our feelings and identities.

In an interview for Instituto Claro, in the series #PensadoresTIC, on November 22, 2013 (http://tinyurl.com/mrjf8al), digital researcher Martha Gabriel talks about hybridity and the way the public behaves on the internet. Gabriel believes that today, with the help of technological developments and the increased use of mobile devices, we have become ON and OFF individuals, unlike in the past, where we had to go to a certain place to connect with each other, this is no longer necessary, as we have devices and internet available practically 24 hours a day, so we can be connected all the time and thus, as has already been said, in a way, be in more than one place at the same time.

From the moment we have the opportunity to be connected in any place where people socialize, we also have the opportunity to find out about certain subjects, for example, in a conversation where you don't understand a subject very well, you just have to go to specialized search sites, such as *Google*[16] and find out about it, What this ON and OFF relationship that Gabriel talks about means is that the way we interact with each other is much easier today than it was a long time ago, all because of this new way of living with the internet and the people who surround you while you're online or offline.

Continuing his thought, Gabriel also believes that due to this ON and OFF relationship, off-line relationships have their days numbered, explaining it better: the fact that we are always distant even though we are close to each other has meant that this type of interaction has lost its essence, so to speak, which makes online relationships more interesting, mainly because of the practical forms of interaction and how they take place between individuals.

> We no longer need to leave where we are to access a machine that takes us to the ON. Today, and increasingly, the ON is with us wherever we are and will soon be connected directly to our brain. So all the major trends in communication and marketing are wonderfully contaminated with ON and OFF integration - transmedia storytelling, social networks, video, search, augmented reality, cloud computing, crowdsourcing, geo-location, real time, and everything else, it's a constant dance between the ON and OFF that make up our daily lives, our lives, (GABRIEL, 2012.).

With this, we can understand that each individual sees the world according to what they believe, for example, just as there is no such thing as pure reality, there is no such thing as pure digital either, in which case each thing is influenced according to the perceptions of each user of cyberspace. This is clear from Gabriel's explanation that the ON is everywhere and will soon be connected to our own brains, making the connection about the different types of thoughts that end up influencing the way individuals act and, at the same time, make them react in different ways in a unified system, Recuero also addresses this issue in his study, when he states that the network is an individual system, where each of its members takes on different roles, where multiple facets of their identity are represented, yet still reaching a whole, that is, despite being individualistic, the process reaches individuals as a whole, and may or may not be productive for each one.

Before addressing hybridity, we will first exemplify its definition, which, according to Martha, is nothing more than the union of the hybrid with the cyber-peresgo, in other words, we, as hybrid individuals, who have different ways of thinking and acting, become part of a reality that is different from what we have experienced before.

Still in this vein, Gabriel sees Internet users as a large number of cybrids, because everything we live and share on the net is part of who we are, the identity we create throughout our existence, and combining the thoughts of Canclini (1999) and Gabriel (2012), it is from this exchange of identities between hybrid beings that new identities and attitudes are formed within the

[16] Google: A multinational online search engine and software company from the United States.

cyberspace, in other words, it is through the influence that each being exerts on the other that the roles of the actors in the network are molded according to what is exposed to this group of people.

Following this train of thought, it is difficult to identify which people belong to certain groups, or even what kind of groups they are, because research becomes more specific. After all, there is no way to define an audience demographically, for example, because although they are in different places, they are both connected in the same space and their thoughts diverge and meet within the same environment. Each user ends up acquiring elements of each other's identity, becoming a person with different attitudes, even divergent on some points, but this relationship is what gives the internet the reach it has with its users.

> The age of connection is the age of mobility. Wireless internet, sentient objects and the latest generation of mobile telephony raise new questions about public space and private space, such as the privatization of public space (where are we when we connect to the internet in a plague or when we talk on our cell phone in the midst of the multitude of streets?), privacy (we will increasingly leave traces of our daily journeys), social relations in groups with smart mobs, etc. The new forms of wireless communication are redefining the use of the space of place and the space of flows (Castells, 1996). In contemporary cities, the traditional spaces of place (streets, squares, avenues, monuments) are gradually being transformed into spaces of flows, flexible, communicational spaces, "digital places" (HORAN, 2000) and (LEMOS, 2005, p. 4).

According to André Lemos (2005), we can understand precisely these changes in the behavior of network users, and also the way in which people act not only online, but also offline, and how digital influences people's lives outside the internet, which follows the same thinking of Gabriel (2012) who relates the ON and OFF experience of individuals. In this way, it is possible to better understand the relationship between society on and off the net, even though both are connected.

Lemos (2005) also talks about the exposure we suffer due to the widespread use of the internet, especially in relation to sharing personal information such as images, videos or even the famous Facebook *statuses,* for example, because posts like these are stored in your history, which makes it easier to find out information about individuals who often don't even remember or are unaware that they are there, It is also understood that this type of attitude is currently considered normal, because from the moment an individual publishes something on a broadband, the intention is for this content to be seen and preferably shared and consequently viewed by even more users.

3.2. FACTORS THAT INDUCE THE SHARING AND SEARCH FOR INFORMATION IN THE FACE OF USERS' NEED FOR RECOGNITION.

According to the study on online consumer behavior, profile, internet use and attitudes, by Maurício Morgado (2003), the image below shows us the type of content that users most look for when connecting to the net.

We can see the kinds of benefits that the Internet brings to users, as well as what they are looking for and why they are looking for it, because from the moment an individual connects, they are no longer just a thinking head but a message propagator, messages that vary in content countless times, but whether they are utilitarian or hedonic, they serve the social development of the network.

Figure 02: Internet use and motivations

Utility benefits	Hedonic benefits
- communication	▪ fun
▪ search for information	▪ pass the time
▪ convenience	- relaxation
▪ economic factors	▪ socializing with friends
	▪ participate in communities

Source: Online consumer behavior: profile, Internet use and attitudes. By: Mauricio Morgado.

Firstly, we understand both the benefits of using the web as sensory stimuli, which in turn involve the consumer and induce psychological factors, also known as internal factors, which are motivation, perception, learning and attitude; and external factors, which are personal, socio-group and cultural factors. These stimuli arise from the use of online platforms as a means of interaction and information between users, in this case, because of the reason that leads each individual to connect and more, to delve deeper into an advertisement, for example, and following this thought, the hedonic benefits, induced by mainly external factors, will be addressed, for example, where the individual seeks through the Internet the acceptance of a certain group or even of himself.

This is commonly seen on social networks, for example, where individuals interact with each other in a more direct way, which ends up increasing their level of knowledge within this environment. This happens through shares and even the famous likes, because it is through these attitudes that other users in common will be able to see what has been published, and the more popularity they get, The better, it's a way of satisfying this new type of consumer, the individual who likes to be seen and who likes to express what they think. What really motivates the relationships between Internet users on the web is mainly this type of publication, those that generate emotions, whether they are of discomfort or happiness, there will always be someone to leave their opinion on matters of this kind.

As mentioned above, everything that generates posts, whatever they may be, reaches a greater number of profiles than other types of posts, and this is because of the socio-cultural changes we are going through.

> With the advent of the internet, new mechanisms have been created for those looking to become celebrities or at least become known. An example of this is the use of social

> networks - Facebook, Twitter and Orkut, among others - by aspiring celebrities who want to achieve their fifteen minutes of fame - predicted by Andy Warhol in 1960 - by using these tools. These networks, which emerged primarily as an agent for social integration, create an environment conducive to exhibitionism and voyeurism, where being contemplated is what matters (OCTAVIANO, 2011).

According to Carolina Octaviano, a journalist who graduated from PUC Campinas and has a post-graduate degree in scientific journalism (2011), with the help of the internet, individuals have found new ways of making themselves known and she gives the example of social networks, following the thought of fifteen minutes of fame already predicted in the past by Andy Warhol (1960), a priori, networks emerged with the aim of facilitating communication and interaction between one individual and another, But with the increase in the number of users, a new form of interaction was created, the form of exhibitionism and voyeurism that Carolina also mentions in her text, in other words, the intention of these people is to attract the attention of other users, to be observed, thus achieving the longed-for recognition, or rather, those fifteen minutes of fame.

These are the hedonic benefits of the internet, many of which are driven by the fact that they want to be in the spotlight, in this case, and also as a form of pleasure and leisure, sharing information with friends and other individuals on the platforms they use. In this way, we can see the different relationships that Internet users have with cyberspace and how these relationships and behaviors have been changing as the network and people have evolved. Based on this, we will also analyze the profile of the utilitarian benefits, which are more focused on receiving productive information.

These benefits can be recognized as the act of carrying out study research, for example, as well as market research, such as those in which the consumer looks for information on a particular product, information media such as online magazines and newspapers, in short, just like leisure, the Internet also has its productive content, which has always been present along with the other wonders it can provide, What remains to be done is to go in search of what is productive, using the network in a more intelligent and effective way for the life of each user, because let's see, if we live in a time when ON and OFF go hand in hand, it is possible, according to Gabriel (2012), that ON often stands out in relation to OFF and it is necessary to be prepared for the consequences of these behaviors that end up generating this "confusion" between ON and OFF.

Users are increasingly demanding in terms of the information they receive, and these users who use the utilitarian benefits are the ones who are most concerned about the content they acquire, so they fit the new consumer profile from the moment that the search for information about the market and relevant content becomes part of their research. They see the Internet as a way of communicating, not only between individuals, but also as a means of reaching companies, for example, through complaints or questions that may be of interest to them.

The "utilitarian benefits" encompass a broader type of user profile. Of course, these users of utilitarian content can also be included in the profile of users of hedonic benefits, because as soon as you are connected, you are exposed to a lot of information, the difference is that, in certain situations, the use of the Internet will be more beneficial and in others not so much, although interaction between users of the network is of paramount importance, not only for the network but for all the other individuals and companies that are included in that medium.

Therefore, the current difficulty is not obtaining information, but what to do with the information that users find, in other words, it is essential to understand that it is not just because you are connected to the net that means you are obtaining information, on the contrary, there is a big difference between productive information and unnecessary information, so to speak, the type of information that is of interest to the growth of the individual is that which comes with something productive, and this is what many users, consumers, have been doing on the Internet, which gives them an extremely important role for the Brazilian digital market, the growth of prosumers on the network makes companies and agencies pay more attention to what is being published by the public and potential clients.

3.3. THE POWER OF CONSUMERS IN THE DIGITAL MARKETPLACE

By defining the profile of the new consumer and the way in which these individuals act on the Internet, we can understand that the relationship between company and customer has been changing over time and this new way of interacting with each other is mainly influenced by the way in which these consumers have been acting, allowing us to observe the great power of influence they have in relation to companies and the most effective ways of remaining integrated in the market and at the same time pleasing as many consumers as possible.

With the advent of the Internet there have been countless behavioral changes and, for the digital market, the most relevant is the way in which consumers act in the online space, because, through technological revolutions, these users are increasingly present in the digital scenario, that is, According to Kotler (2010), companies need to reinvent themselves every day, especially in relation to the strategies they use to bring their customers closer together, inducing them to interact with the company.

According to Lipovetsky, commercial exchanges are not merely economic, but represent a search for an ideal, for a form of identification in the world (Lipovetsky apud VIEIRA, 2011, p. 7 - 8). In other words, with this in mind, individuals consume in order to keep themselves in the spotlight within society and the groups to which they belong.

Companies take advantage of this feeling by making their products even more visible through advertisements on the Internet. Customers themselves advertise companies because, just as they can use the Internet to complain, they also play a very important role, which is that of a satisfied consumer, in this case, the so-called prosumer, who will publish and share information or products from certain companies, praising the quality of their product or service, This is why customer relations are so important for a company's growth and this goes beyond the digital landscape. After all, we are no longer just ON or OFF, we are ON and OFF and everything that happens ON has repercussions on OFF and vice versa.

> Today, the bomb has dropped. Citizens who feel aggrieved when they receive a service or product don't hesitate to speak out. And they often do so loudly. They ignore the representatives appointed by the company and the communication channels it has set up. They prefer to complain to the whole world at once. They use specialized websites and social networks. Their voice shakes even the biggest companies. The impact of this new consumer power to destroy reputations is revolutionizing the way companies deal with their public (CORONATO, 2013).

According to Marcos and Mauro (2013), both from Época magazine, "the bomb has dropped", and this can be explained by the fact that current consumer behavior means that any and all dissatisfaction with a service or product is a reason to speak out, and usually through social networks. It can also be seen that this is often done with a lot of fanfare, which ends up having very unsatisfactory consequences for these representatives, and this type of attitude has ended up changing the way companies see and treat their customers.

This way, consumers are there, ready to claim their rights. This also happens with the help of specialized sites such as "Reclame Aqui" (http://www.reclameaqui.com.br/), which even has an app for mobile devices and was created especially for those dissatisfied consumers who are looking for attention about what they are unhappy with. In Época magazine's report on consumer power (http://tinyurl.com/ldorvfn), this type of action is explained and evaluated in relation to what companies are doing to circumvent and mold themselves to the new profile of their public.

Figure 03: Image from the Reclame Aqui website.

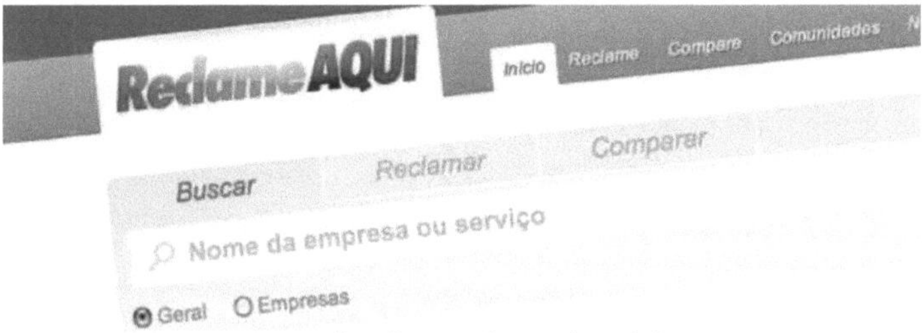

Source: (http://www.reclameaqui.com.br/).

Figure 04: Image of the Reclame Aqui application.

Source: (http://www.reclameaqui.com.br/).

In addition to having several options for comparing products and companies, complaining about a company, service or product, among other items available on the site, there is also a ranking of the companies with the most complaints. The "Reclame Aqui" website also has a link to recent complaints, answered complaints and evaluated complaints. And on its page, consumers have the opportunity to follow the situation not only of their own problems but also of those of other people who are dissatisfied like them, in other words, the site is a great communication tool between company and consumer, because, based on what is explicit there, it is possible for the company to take action to improve its services, and consequently make its customers happy.

A report by "Brainstorm9" (http://tinyurl.com/muaxbmr) shows a study carried out by Facebook in partnership with the Ipsos Institute, which looks at the amount of engagement the Latin American public has on the Internet, with the result that Brazilians are the ones who interact most with brands, celebrities and personalities via social networks. According to the survey, 67% of Brazilians interviewed say they are influenced by brands or friends' actions on Facebook, 44% like brands or companies on social networks and 41% read what companies post, and just behind the Brazilians are the Mexicans in 2nd place.

Graph 05: Latin Americans on Facebook and interaction with brands.

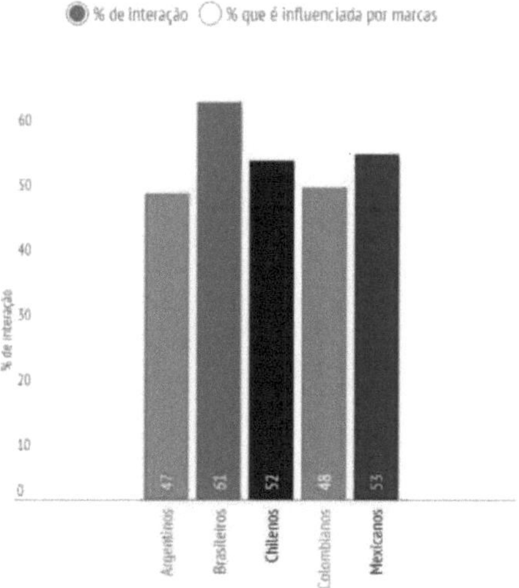

Source: "Facebook reach and usage", Ipsos MediaCT. (http://tinyurl.com/muaxbmr) Accessed in: 2014.

One example of this interaction is the ways that consumers find to reach their brands, such as the example of a young man called Pedro Tessarolo, who directs a post on Twitter to two sporting goods brands, Netshoes and Centauro, where he says that he would like to buy a product but that it has the same price in both stores and wants to know what they will do to help him. As in the example below:

Figure 05: Consumer vs. Company interaction.

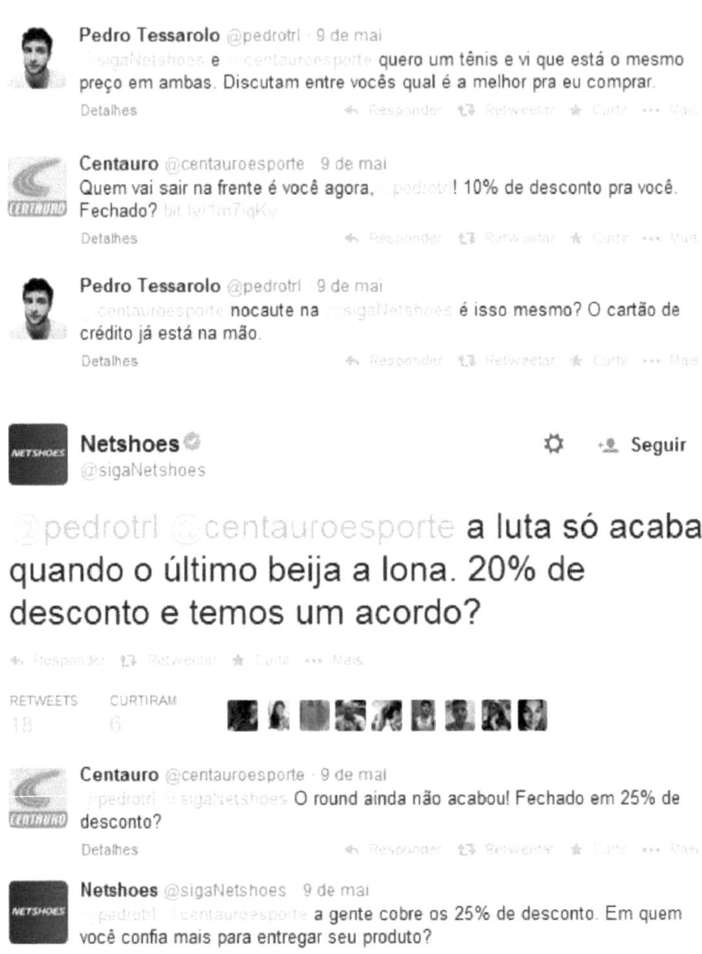

Source: (http://tinyurl.com/mxyjyj8), Accessed in: 2014.

There remains a question pertinent to this relationship of power that the consumer has with companies: After all, what is the fate of companies in relation to the power exercised by the new consumer profile?

Consumers are becoming increasingly demanding and participative, especially when something is bothering them and making them dissatisfied,

It is therefore the role of companies to know how to deal with the situation and what to do to reverse it, because even the biggest of companies can have its reputation thrown into the toilet by the publication of a dissatisfied consumer, and before trying to reverse any situation, it is necessary to create a bond with the customer, precisely in order to generate more affinity so that unpleasant situations don't happen.

> Brand identity has to do with its positioning in the minds of consumers. For your brand to be heard and noticed in a tumultuous market, it needs to have a unique positioning. It also needs to be relevant to consumers' rational needs and desires. (KOTLER, 2010. p. 41)

Kotler (2010) believes that a brand needs to have a unique positioning in the market, because this is how it will attract its audience and, above all, build loyalty, as well as planning actions that are strategically designed to meet the interests of its audience, always seeking innovations in line with their needs and market demands, not to mention the way it interacts with its audience, creating specialized platforms for this type of service, because the more special the consumer feels, the better for the company's image.

In other words, consumers have been shaped by society and by cyber changes and have ended up molding companies to their behavior. You have to know how to act and when to act in the face of a platform that is constantly changing like the internet, and also in the face of consumers who are also constantly changing and who say and do what they want, so to speak, participating more actively in the process as consumers, or rather prosumers, who share and expose their anxieties to companies and the persistent issues of life.

It's no wonder that the Brazilian digital market is one of the fastest-growing in recent years, and this data only proves the strength it is gaining with the passage of time and technological revolutions. The public is more communicative and participative in relation to companies, brands and everything that is happening in the world, everything is shared and everything is seen and published. And it is on this basis that agencies and companies must position themselves, keeping up with what the media is imposing and always reinventing themselves.

The next chapter will analyze some agencies in the city of Belém and the way they have been behaving in the face of these issues and how this consumer behavior and the new way of consuming influences the positioning of agencies and how they work within companies.

4. RESEARCH METHODOLOGY

Considering what has been analyzed in the previous chapters, this research basically aims to show the major recurring changes in society's attitude and, above all, how the changes that individuals have undergone have started to interfere in the market and in the way in which agencies/companies are interacting with their audiences. From the social and behavioral changes of individuals connected to the Internet came the instrument for analyzing the work, which seeks, through research carried out in the metropolitan region of Belém, to better understand how the digital market works in our state, also understanding how it has been consolidating itself and generating more opportunities for the segment.

According to Sylvia Vergara's (2003) research methods, this study can be classified as descriptive and explanatory research. According to Vergara, descriptive research is based on the process of describing and analyzing content related to aspects of society's interaction and the means these individuals use to communicate and be closer to each other, while explanatory research is represented precisely by the factors that affect and, in turn, end up influencing these individuals and, with them, the market as well.

Based on Vergara's thinking, the research can be understood in these two ways, which were carried out through a bibliographical survey and scientific study and also through research carried out according to the inductive method, which, according to Eva Maria Lakatos (2003), takes place through induction about what is being researched, In this case, understanding that users have changed over the course of the Internet's evolution and have consequently influenced the advertising market through their new way of behaving, the research is based on what each agency surveyed had to do and rethink about its services so that it could remain within the Pará market.

> Induction is a mental process by means of which, starting from particular data, sufficiently verified, a general or universal truth is inferred, not contained in the parts examined. Therefore, the aim of inductive arguments is to lead to conclusions whose content is much broader than that of the premises on which they are based (LAKATOS, 2003, p 86.).

Following on from this thought, and exemplifying what has been mentioned above, the inductive method is the way to reach conclusions through data and from what has been happening according to the course of what is made explicit in the scientific study of the research, which happens mainly through the explanatory research cited by Vergara (2003), This case study is based on a survey of three agencies in the city of Belém do Pará, with the aim of understanding the influence of the new consumer profile on the advertising market in the region and also to identify whether the city is keeping pace with the growth of the digital market as well as Brazil, given that the number of users is increasing and will continue to do so.

The study was carried out over a period of three months, during which time the subject and object of the study were chosen, which, once the content had been developed, could be made more specific. During this time, data and resources were also collected and surveys carried out with three agencies in the state. These surveys were carried out within an average of one month, by e-mail with representatives or employees from specific areas of these agencies.

Three agencies were chosen for the research, the first being CA Comunicagao, where the research was carried out with the Digital Platform Marketing Analyst, Philippe Medeiros. The second agency is Yesbil Comunicagao Digital, where the research was carried out with José Calazans, who was formerly responsible for the execution and planning of social media monitoring projects, and who continues to collaborate with ideas and content. And the third and final agency is Eko Estratégias em Comunicagao, with Corporate Communications and Press Office Analyst Josiele Soeiro.

Each of the agencies was chosen precisely because they have different roles, which, although complete, have more specific areas, which are more prominent within the agency and also with its clients. Another important factor in choosing the agencies is the different positioning they each have in relation to the consumer and the market, i.e. the main objective is to compare the way these agencies work and show that even with similar work, they have different and specific profiles at certain points.

4.1. CA COMMUNICATION

Figure 06: CA Communication logo

Source: Agency website, Available at: https://www.facebook.com/CAcomunicacaoON7frefMs

CA Comunicado is an agency that has been on the market for 27 years and describes itself as an innovative agency, born out of communication, unlike other agencies on the market that began to define themselves as a communication agency after CA's first step, which, according to its biography, was a pioneer in this area. Referring to its clients as its idols, CA reinforces the idea of sentimentality towards its clients, showing that they are the key to the growth and recognition of its team's work.

Over the course of its almost three decades, CA has innovated by creating a company of its own, CA No Media, which specializes in press relations, events, promotional campaigns and all things media. The agency also has CA Interativa, which came into being even before CA No Media, and which has completed 10 years in the Pará market. In the research (Appendix I) carried out with Medeiros, CA can be seen as a complete agency, with medium and large sectors, capable of meeting the demands of the current digital market and, above all, its clients.

Identifying its "restlessness" stance, the agency shows that it is always looking for innovations in its work so that it becomes more and more complete, thus having the opportunity to grow and solidify itself even more in the market. As CA's main focus is its clients, the agency started to integrate the digital sector after the great demand for services requested specifically for this area, and what until a certain time was limited to services such as the placement of digital handles on portals and platforms now has an exclusive area focused solely on digital.

According to Medeiros (Appendix I), the sector exclusively for digital was implemented in 2014, when they identified the need to hire a professional to help with the demands, based on the needs of clients such as GM (Chevrolet), and following this course, CA also started to provide services such as running ads on various platforms, monitoring, using analytics tools and also carrying out studies based on performance and research.

In response to a question in the survey asking what the demand is and what kind of service is most sought after at the agency, Medeiros says that just like one of his biggest clients, GM, the other clients also feel the need to stay in the spotlight on digital platforms, although there is a certain amount of fear on their part, because, the digital market in the city is still in its infancy and clients still have this fear, due to a lack of knowledge of the benefits that the sector can bring to their businesses. However, Medeiros says that they try to encourage their clients to run audiovisual ads on YouTube, all of which is always based on and proposed through research and analysis of consumer profile and demand.

Always seeking to reinvent itself and keep up with the demands of our market, the CA Comunicagao agency shows an innovative profile, which in turn differs from more traditional agencies and even from the other agencies mentioned in this research, with a more personal positioning, which is easily seen in the agency's description on its website (Available at: http://cacomunicacao.com.br/), which talks about itself in a somewhat colloquial and easily assimilated language, which is one of the great moves of companies that are inserted in the digital market today, to deal with the public in the way you would with a close friend, for example.

"Currently I believe we are looking for synergy between off and online communication. " (Appendix I) Following this train of thought, we can identify CA as a complete agency, seeking new horizons and following the flow of the state's advertising market as a whole, whether online or offline.

> I hope every day that the culture of the 'TV, Radio, Newspaper Campaign' ends and that Pará's entrepreneurs take the plunge without fear, but with responsibility and care, into proposing 'Hybrid Campaigns', with transmedia, perhaps even crossmedia and ads that solve problems and exalt values. Between you and me, we're already saturated, we want to be surprised. (Appendix I, MEDEIROS, 2014)

The above quote shows the concern, or rather the hope, that Medeiros has for the digital market, addressing the means used by this segment, comparing them to traditional media and trying to show their importance in today's advertising environment, we live in an age where everyone is connected to everything that is involved with the internet and especially the agile means of communication, and the agency sees this, this need to be inserted assiduously in the market and especially in the Bethlehem cycle, because they believe that this is a sector that only tends to grow and solidify itself every day. With the aim of innovating the image of the advertising market in Pará, opening up opportunities for new demands and new ways of reaching clients.

As a result, the agency maintains its engagement in the market, always seeking to innovate and add attributes to its services, such as CA no media, which was created by the company exclusively to meet the demand of clients looking for innovations, especially those involving the digital market, and this has only grown and encouraged the company to grow more and more, which is different from the agency we analyze below, which originated focused on digital.

4.2. YESBIL DIGITAL COMMUNICATION

Figure 07: Yesbil Digital Communication logo.

Source: Agency website (Available at: https://www.facebook.com/Yesbil?fref=ts).

Yesbil began its digital journey in Pará in March 2010. Focused specifically on this sector of the market, the agency already believed in the segment's great potential within advertising, foreseeing not only its growth worldwide, but especially in the state of Pará, and it was from this expectation that the agency remained in the market, always seeking to pass on what it was experiencing as professional learning, but also always recycling itself, and in these four years of life, Yesbil has prioritized its activities in the development of websites and online systems, brand management and content production for websites and social media.

Although it has already been operating in the market for four years, the agency has become more prominent in the last two years, when it took the initiative to produce lectures and courses aimed at professionals in the digital area. Yesbil currently uses the positioning that "Sharing knowledge is life", based on this, the agency seeks to further improve its courses and lectures so that those interested in its services can obtain more information and clear up doubts in relation to the state's digital market.

> Today the company relates to two audiences: students/professionals and company directors/owners. Each audience requires a different content strategy. Students demand courses and lectures, business owners demand more detailed posts and market studies. There is an e-mail base where we send different content to each audience. This helps us to go beyond social networks. (Appendix II, CALAZANS. 2014)

This is precisely because Yesbil now has two positions: That is, with this initiative of giving lectures and courses, the company gained more knowledge, consequently attracting more customers for its other types of services, and so Yesbil makes its stance very evident on its web platform (Available at: http://www.yesbil.com/sobre/), where it exposes its entrepreneurial and visionary behavior regarding the issue of the market and the propagation of information about the state's digital sector.

Figure 08: Yesbil Digital Communication website

Source: (http://www.yesbil.com/sobre/) Accessed in: 2014.

For Calazans (Appendix II), the public has become increasingly mature, mainly due to the fact that the internet is not exactly a medium sought out only for the purpose of doing business or consuming, but for personal use, which in turn is extremely important for companies and agencies, because it is from there that the relationship with the client takes on another aspect, as has been said before, the profile of today's consumer is that type of public that needs attention and, above all, needs to feel important, In contrast, just like Medeiros (2014), Calazans (2014) also sees that there is still a lack of understanding on the part of companies about digital in our region, the lack of investment is one of the factors that most contributes to the market moving at a slow pace, because companies are somewhat suspicious about the results of this type of service.

"Communication is learning that you can't do anything without thinking about digital, even if it's just a video that will be shown on TV. It always has implications for user behavior on the web." (Appendix II, Calazans). With this statement, we can understand what was said earlier in the study, because since the emergence of the Internet and its evolution, the way in which individuals interact and behave in society has changed and changed along with the network, because with it, individuals have the opportunity to be connected at all times, even more so if we talk about technological revolutions and the number of new technologies.

smartphone and mobile internet users, the fact that they are all connected means that offline media such as TV are going through some changes, even what is shown on TV ends up going online, in other words, this relationship is the reality of the current way consumers act.

With a distinctive stance on the market, Yesbil says its mission is to "Constantly Renew and Share Knowledge", also showing itself to be a company concerned with the roots of our state and our culture in Pará, its focus and way of working with clients is what makes its services and especially its lectures and courses attract a lot of attention from an audience that is always connected and attentive to changes in the market and the society we live in, with a more relaxed and relaxed language, looking at the agency's website we have the feeling that we are in a simple conversation with friends, which is somewhat similar to the positioning of CA Comunicação.

Although similar, the agencies have different experiences and sectors, as we can see, CA, unlike Yesbil, has already created its sector after its growth and demand, unlike Yesbil, which has specialized in this since its first steps, it is clear that over time both agencies have matured and solidified in the market, conquering their place in Belém's digital scene, which differs somewhat from the other agencies, given that their specialty is advisory work.

4.2. EKO COMMUNICATION STRATEGIES

Figure 09: Eko Strategies in Communication logo

Source: Agency website (Available at: https://www.facebook.com/agenciaeko?fref=ts.) Accessed in: 2014.

Eko is an agency that has partnerships with professionals and other agencies in states such as Pará, Amazonas, Amapá, Roraima, Rondonia, Acre and Maranháo; and its work aims to offer integrated communication solutions for companies and organizations, specializing in communication strategies in the Amazon. One of the agency's main sectors is press relations, which has solid business knowledge and uses this to achieve success in its work and to better understand what its client needs, based on the well-known prestige and crisis indicators, as the company itself says on its website (Available at: http://www.ekonet.com. br/).

> The work of the press office goes far beyond producing press releases or scheduling interviews: we always create opportunities so that the client is always in the media and well positioned, of course. Scenario reading is fundamental to this process. We monitor newspapers, websites, clients' competition and business opportunities on a daily basis in order to develop better strategies. The press office is essential for any company today, as it

> is responsible for keeping the client's image positive with the press and other opinion formers. (Appendix III, SOEIRO. 2014)

In an interview, Soeiro (Appendix III) discusses the agency's advisory sector, which is considered to be one of Eko's main sectors, specializing in advising large companies in the state, they see this segment in a broader and obviously more differentiated way, They always invest in knowledge of their audience and the scenario in which their client will be inserted, showing that, unlike the other agencies analyzed, Eko has its differential in press relations, and with this, they affirm that this type of service is fundamental for companies, because it is from press relations that the company's image will always remain positive.

One of its main characteristics is the use of regional roots, showing itself to be an agency from the region that has the intention of passing on information to the most varied states without losing its regionality and cultural character, "after all, living surrounded by Amazonian echoes means passing on images, traits and concepts that increasingly arouse international interest" (Available at: http://www.ekonet.com.br/), in other words, the agency uses regionality as an inspiration, and this can be seen in some of its work, even in the way it is positioned on its website, showing that the cultural beauties of each of the states it has partnerships with are relevant to the development of its name and brand, attracting a certain amount of public attention from this, because individuals like to feel part of what is published in the media, whether online or offline.

According to Josiele Soeiro (Appendix III), the agency is always attentive to the changes and demands of the market, which is why, with the growing popularity of the digital sector in the region, Eko began to adapt its advisory service in conjunction with digital marketing, using joint strategies to better serve its clientele, Bearing in mind that the digital sector is the big boom in today's market, bringing these two sectors together has been crucial to the agency's success, which is currently one of the company's most sought-after areas, where most clients maintain both advisory and digital marketing accounts. Soeiro (2014) also believes that this integration is increasingly necessary in our daily lives.

> We see every client as an opportunity. And also a constant challenge. Each client has a different profile, we serve companies from various segments ranging from the mining sector, hospitals to shopping malls, so each one has an objective ("what to communicate? To whom? In what way?). (Appendix III, SOEIRO. 2014)

From the above quote, it can be understood that, for the agency, the client is its main concern, because it is through the relationship with the client that Eko will be able to know what needs to be done and the best way to do it, according to what is being requested on its website, The agency emphasizes that it sends "the right message to each audience", through its briefing work with its clients and also through targeted research into each client's profile, a relationship that is essential for both parties to understand each other and, as a result, the success of the service offered.

"Eko's role is to offer communication solutions to these companies in order to strengthen and preserve their image." (Appendix III, Soeiro), the client's image is what is most evident in the process of advising a company, and Eko seeks to strengthen this image, through, of course, specialized communication strategies aimed at this sector, which, when combined with digital marketing, as mentioned above, reaches even greater proportions, thus giving the agency due recognition.

Although it has only been on the market for a short time, Eko is already very popular, and this popularity is due precisely to the company's regional positioning, which sets it apart from the others on the market, like the other two agencies analyzed in the study, where they differ not only in their activities in the various sectors of an agency, but also in their positioning in relation to their clients.

4.4. SOME CONSIDERATIONS ABOUT THE ROLE OF AGENCIES

By analyzing and comparing the companies studied in this case, we can see that they are very similar to each other. Although they operate more specifically in different sectors, both Eko and Ca have a complete agency system, which differs only from Yesbil, which operates exclusively in the digital sector, However, it also has some similarities with the other agencies, similarities that can be seen in the image that each passes on to its public. For example, CA and Yesbil are more similar in their relaxed communication, while Eko's message is direct and more formal, as can be seen on their respective websites.

It is also understood that just as Kotler (2010) says that it is from digital marketing strategies, or the so-called marketing 3.0, that companies will have the opportunity to interact with the public in a more direct and personal way, and with the help of the internet it has become visibly easier to unveil their aspirations and thus satisfy their desires, through exactly this type of strategy used by companies, the attitude of seeking to understand through planning and monitoring the profile of each consumer and from this to know what each one wants.

Thus, each of the agencies analyzed has specific positions, for example Yesbil, which was created with the digital market in mind, which at the time was taking small steps in the region, but which nevertheless already foresaw a promising future for the segment, opening up the way for more agencies in the same field, and differentiating Yesbil from the other agencies already present in the market, which at the time, due to a lack of resources and manpower, was unable to carry out the same offline media work as the other agencies, so it invested and took advantage of the growth of digital in the state and especially the growth in popularity of online advertising and the number of users on the web.

CA Comunicagao, on the other hand, although it has some similarities with Yesbil, began its work primarily with the offline media and advisory sector, and over time and due to market demands, it was necessary to implement the digital sector, which although small, met the demands of its clients for a while, But with the growth of technologies and especially the ways in which people interact with the internet, and consequently the increase in demand and requirements from clients, a department was set up exclusively for this type of strategy, which is the aforementioned Ca No Media, which has been in existence for ten years and is focused on the agency's digital strategies.

Eko's positioning is more different from the others, because with a more formal and direct language, the agency shows its regional side and also the close relationship it has with its clients, always aiming for the well-being and satisfaction of its public, also highlighting its work with events, digital marketing, consultancy and institutional communication, all work with a regional character, showing the culture of each state where the agency is located, in addition to diversifying its services for the most varied clients, ranging from hospitals to shopping malls.

All the agencies surveyed are aware of the importance and growth of the digital market in the region, they also believe that the market is promising and that their services will only grow, judging by the way the public deals with online media, not to mention the position of each one with regard to the public, where it is always evident that the client is the main tool for the success of their work.

By analyzing the research carried out with the three agencies, it was possible to see the similarities in their thinking about the Belem market, but mainly the differences and each other's needs, for example:

> The regional digital market is still in its infancy. In addition to the market being very immature, we have very few (really) qualified professionals. Clients and agencies are aware of the importance of digital media, but they don't invest in the qualification of their employees and they don't allocate a portion of the campaign budget to investments in digital media. (Appendix II, CALAZANS. 2014)

In other words, based on this principle and the analysis of each of the agencies that believe in the digital market as an exciting segment, which is clearly growing and taking its place, but which, in Belém, is still taking short steps, However, in Belém it is still taking short steps, but it is growing with the passage of time and especially with these new forms of interaction, not only between people but also between people and the internet and everything that this online world offers them, ranging from the most up-to-date information to the oldest information, everyone is recycling themselves, innovating not only technologies and media but also the minds of each individual who is inserted in cyberspace.

Through this study it was possible to observe that, as all agencies believe, the digital market is the current major focus within the city of Belém, where agencies that don't have a digital sector are beginning to adapt to the enterprise, not to mention the number of digital agencies that are being created, which means that there is an increase in demand for the service and even recognition as well, Despite the fact that the digital market in Belém is still scarce, resources are only increasing and with them the number of clients, because the greater the volume of demand, the more this segment will solidify, that is, in Belém, it is necessary to invest more and even better adapt some agencies so that the service becomes more effective and promising.

FINAL CONSIDERATIONS

With this work, it was possible to better understand how cyberculture and cyberspace remain present in our daily lives, or rather, how individuals keep them present, and how this technological and cybernetic revolution has influenced the behavior of web users and consequently the "real" lives of these individuals.

The work can be understood as a reference to the cultural and behavioral changes in society since the existence of the first computer, better known as a programmable machine, up to the present day with the large number of access options and, above all, the expansion of this access, This is precisely because of the way in which the Internet has entered the homes and lives of Brazilian society, and it seems that it is here to stay and will not stop where it is. Research has also shown that this is a phenomenon that is of paramount importance to the economy, both in terms of the technology market and the market as a whole, because with its ease of use, Internet users have access to more and more things, and more and more quickly.

The importance of the web for the market is not just due to the fact that it has increased the consumption of devices that allow access to the Internet, but rather the way in which it has boosted the online market and purchases made over the Internet, not to mention the increased interaction between individuals and companies, the relationship between product and consumer has become closer, The relationship between product and consumer has become closer, more personal, and this is one of the factors that leads these users to make purchases or to complain or praise a company or product/service that is available. Customer care has had to be doubled, after all, the prosumer only needs seconds to end or boost the popularity of a company or service.

The influence of the new consumer profile is also a factor to pay attention to, because it was based on this new type of behavior that companies began to better see what the customer wanted and, moreover, to better prepare themselves to position themselves in the digital market, and above all, Being part of the digital market as an entrepreneur is essential, because even traditional media such as TV are already losing ground to this new segment, precisely because it's so easy, because people can watch what they want and when they want, without having to follow a program; on the contrary, it's all on the fly, at the same moment.

As a result, consumers have started to behave in a more incisive and demanding way, because everyone wants to and will fight for their rights, whether they are right or not, everything is a reason to share or expose their ideas, especially when something is not to their liking and then in a matter of seconds, a post is shared by thousands of people and it doesn't matter if they are your friends on social networks, what matters is the number of users who will be reached, and the more, the better. This kind of attitude happens because of the need to be seen by the users connected to the network. After all, if the individual doesn't want their photo to be seen, they won't publish it on a social network that has millions of people connected and that their friends' friends can access without them even knowing.

Following this thought, we enter the argument of Martha Gabriel, who sees Internet users as hybrid beings, who live in the offline and online world, all at the same time and that in a short time this will no longer be distinguished, the possibility of being in two places at the same time makes the individual stop interacting with each other in the same environment to interact online, this is commonly seen among young people, people are increasingly connected and dependent on this great virtual world, and the digital advertising market is realizing a great opportunity in this type of attitude.

Starting from this principle, a study carried out exclusively to understand this process of influence and participation would be considerable since, from this study, I was able to perceive the great influence of this new consumer profile, taking into account the exacerbated growth of the media and the digital market itself, this new relationship between consumers and the Internet is getting closer every day and with each evolution, and I believe that this behavior will still give rise to countless changes in the social space within the network and, above all, in the way in which these individuals relate in the ON and OFF space.

Just as capitalism and the market influence individuals to stay connected as a form of recognition and even self-knowledge, they also make users want more and more news and consequently more work and more profit for the digital market. It's no wonder that the Brazilian digital market grew considerably from 2013 to 2014, because it's through prosumers that online advertising can spread and reach an exorbitant number of individuals and potential customers. Therefore, the influence of this behavior is the main key to market growth.

The digital market in Pará has not been left behind and has been gaining ground too, where more and more agencies are including the digital sector within their companies and reinventing themselves and even changing the way they act with their public, taking on more relaxed attitudes and presenting themselves in a more casual language, seeking to adapt to the demands of the market which, despite moving at a slow pace in the region, has all the potential to become a major segment of the regional advertising market.

REFERENCES

Associapáo Brasileira de Agencias Digitais - Available at: < http://www.abradi.com.br/ > Accessed: September 28, 2014.

Professional Association of Advertising Agencies of the State of Pará - Available at: < http://www.sinapropa.com.br/site/2014/ > Accessed on: October 4, 2014

CA Comunicapáo - Available at: < http://cacomunicacao.com.br/ > Accessed on: November 09, 2014.

CORONATO, Marcos and SILVEIRA, Mauro. 2013. **Never Has the Consumer Had as Much Power as in the Digital Age**, Revista Época. Available at: <http://tinyurl.com/ldorvfn> Access: October 17, 2014.

Eko Estratégias em Comunicapáo - Available at: < http://www.ekonet.com.br/ > Accessed on: November 09, 2014.

FIRMINO, Andreá. **Consumption in Contemporary Society: A reflection on the motives that lead to hedonic consumption.** - Brazilian Society for Interdisciplinary Communication Studies - Intercom. 2010. At: < http://tinyurl.com/lny3wwa > Accessed: October 19, 2014.

GABRIEL, Martha. 2012. **Hybridity: ON and OFF line at the same time.** At: <http://www.martha.com.br/cibridismo-on-e-off-line-ao-mesmo-tempo/> Accessed: October 18, 2014.

GABRIEL, Martha. 2013. **Martha Gabriel talks about the role of the new teacher and the use of ICT in education**, Pensadores TIC. - Available at: <http://tinyurl.com/mrjf8al> Accessed: October 15, 2014.

KOTLER, Philip. **Marketing 3.0**: The Forces That Are Defining the New Human-Centered Marketing. - Ed. Elsevier. 2010.

LAFLOUFA, Jacqueline. **Among Latin Americans, Brazilians engage most with brands on Facebook**, Brainstorm9. - Available at: <http://tinyurl.com/muaxbmr> Accessed: October 22, 2014.

LAURINDO, Roseméri. **"Hybrid Advertising" reflects on new configurations of advertising and analyzes cases.** - Brazilian Society for Interdisciplinary Communication Studies - Intercom. 2012. Available at: < http://www.portcom.intercom.org.br/revistas/index.php/bibliocom/article/viewFile/1206 /1126> Accessed on: October 3, 2014.

LEMOS, André. **Cyberculture and Mobility: The Age of Connection.** - Brazilian Society for Interdisciplinary Communication Studies - Intercom. 2005.

LEVY, Pierre. **Cyberculture**. Sao Paulo: Ed 34, 1999.

MARCONI, Marina e LAKATOS, Eva. **Fundamentals of Scientific Methodology** - Ed. Atlas. 2003.

Social Media in the Enterprise: The Online Relationship with the Market - Deloitte, 2010. Available at: < http://www.deloitte.com/ > Accessed on: October 2, 2014.
MORGADO, Mauricio. **Online consumer behavior: profile, Internet use and attitudes.** - Sao Paulo, 2003.

Online media investment figures. Available at: < http://iabbrasil.net/portal/numeros-de-investimento-em-midia- online/?gclid=CI¡YvZbokMECFRJk7AodBBsApA > Accessed on: September 30, 2014.

OCTAVIANO, Carolina. 2011. **The Fifteen Minutes of Fame and the Spectacularization of Everyday Life.** At: <http://tinyurl.com/mwry6v3> Accessed: October 20, 2014).

Philip Kotler proposes the concept of marketing 3.0 to companies, Exame.com, 2010 - Available at: < http://exame.abril.com.br/marketing/noticias/philip-kotler- propoe-as-empresas-o-conceito-do-marketing-3-0 > Accessed on: October 1, 2014.

Reclame aqui, Website. - Available at: <http://www.reclameaqui.com.br/> Access: October 22, 2014.

RECUERO, Raquel. **Social Networks on the Internet**. Porto Alegre: Ed Meridional, 2009.
Webshoppers Report, 2014- 30ª EDIQÁO. Available at: < http://img.ebit.com.br/webshoppers/pdf/WebShoppers2014 2oSeme.pdf > Accessed on: October 4, 2014.

VERGARA, S.C. **Projetos e relatórios de pesquisa em administrado**. 4. ed. Sao Paulo: Atlas, 2003.
VIEIRA, Manuela. **Consumption in postmodernity: The relationship between identity and communication at the Parintins Festival.** - Identity communication and representation - XI Lusocom Congress, 2011.

VIEIRA, Manuela. **Social networks, identity constructions and consumption processes in post-modernity**. - Thematic Axis Games, Social Networks, Mobility and Urban Communication Structures - V Simposio Nacional da ABCiber.

Yesbil Comunicagáo Digital - Available at: <http://www.yesbil.com/sobre/> Accessed on: November 09, 2014.

APPENDIX I.

Survey conducted with Philippe Medeiros, Digital Platform Marketing Analyst at CA Comunicagao (2014)

1. Can you talk about CA and how the agency works?

CA Comunicagao has been renewing itself in the Pará market for 27 years. The CA group is made up of the CA Comunicagao agency, which handles everything related to advertising and publicity, and CA No Media, which is responsible for press relations, events, promotional campaigns and everything in the media. We have all the sectors of a medium-large agency, from customer service to the archive sector, with a library professional.

2. Why did CA decide to integrate the digital area into the agency?

CA Comunicagao has been working with General Motors (GM - the Chevrolet automaker) for three years, in conjunction with the national and global agency. As a result, CA began to receive demands from GM exclusively for the digital environment. Together with GM's requests, the CEOs began to feel the need to present their clients with digital-focused services.

3. How long has the area been part of the agency?

The exclusive digital department was set up at the beginning of 2014, but the media department was already working on some digital spots on portals and platforms, on behalf of GM (Chevrolet). Today, in addition to running ads on various platforms, we monitor, use analytics tools and carry out studies based on performance and research.

4. Before that, was the digital service outsourced or did the agency not work in this area?

Because of GM, the agency only worked with ads on portals. At that point, the need arose for a digital professional to help with Chevrolet's demands and meet the doubts and needs that clients were already pointing out about the digital environment.

5. How do you work? What is your role within the agency?

At Ca I'm a Marketing Analyst for Digital Platforms. My activities are divided between the demands of GM (Chevrolet) and other clients. For both, I'm responsible for running, monitoring and analyzing ads for Sponsored Links (Google), True-view (Youtube), Social Media (Facebook) and Display Network (Google). In the case of other clients, there is a need to create projects and present them together with the customer service department, draw up digital-focused strategies, media plans and maps, and monitor execution and analysis. Because I don't know the technical side,

I need to provide a basis for the presentations and create projects.

6. How is customer demand, what type of service is most sought after?

As I said earlier, we serve GM, so we have several exclusive demands for the digital sector. The national agency and GM are aware of the brand's need to be present in the digital environment, so the demands are daily and the digital campaigns perennial. Other clients feel the need to be present on social platforms, but there is a certain fear. We also encourage some of our clients to run audiovisual ads on YouTube. Our proposals are always based on research and analysis of digital media.

7. How does the agency position itself in relation to market demands?

We are aligned with the national market. CA has highly qualified professionals who have received advanced training from Google and Facebook professionals. I currently believe that we are seeking synergy between off and online communication.

8. What do you think of the digital market in Belém?

The regional digital market is still in its infancy. In addition to the market being very immature, we have very few (really) qualified professionals. Clients and agencies are aware of the importance of digital media, but they don't invest in the qualification of their employees and they don't allocate a portion of the campaign budget to investments in digital media. Unfortunately, I still come across agencies that label themselves as 'Digital Agencies' or 'Social Media', selling their services for shameful sums, with promises worthy of a braggart politician and guaranteeing great results with very low investments. Many clients and agencies still see digital as a "free" or very cheap vehicle. However, social platforms, search engines, portals, among others, are media that should be given a lot of attention (read attention and attention$$ao), because the ads can be extremely targeted and with much more expressive results than the traditional investment in insertions in Globo's 9 o'clock news. I hope every day that the culture of the 'TV, Radio, Newspaper Campaign' will end and that Pará's entrepreneurs will dive fearlessly, but responsibly and carefully, into proposals for 'Hybrid Campaigns', with transmedia, perhaps even crossmedia and ads that solve problems and exalt values. Between you and me, we're already saturated, we want to be surprised.

APPENDIX II.

Research conducted with José Calazans, Current Collaborator with Idéias e Conteúdo and Former Partner and Coordinator of Monitoring and Content for Social Media at Yesbil Comunicagao Digital. (2014)

1. **How do you work? What is your role within the agency?**

I'm no longer a partner in the company, just a collaborator with ideas and content. When I was still a partner, I coordinated monitoring and content for social media.

I was responsible for the execution and planning of social media monitoring projects. Whether for clients or internal company projects such as the Círio study on Instagram.

2. **Can you talk about Yesbil and how the agency works?**

The company has been on the market for 4 years. It began by offering social media and website creation services and gradually adapted to the needs of the market. Today it works exclusively with social media monitoring, online media planning and digital communication training.

3. **Has Yesbil already been created with digital in mind? If so, why? If not, when did they decide to integrate and why?**

The agency thought about going digital right from the start. The choice came about because it couldn't compete with the other agencies by offering off-site media services. It's much more advantageous to offer the service they don't offer and don't have the structure for than to compete on an equal footing.

4. **How long has the agency been in business?**

It has been doing this for 4 years, but has become more prominent in the last 2 years with the sharing of monitoring studies.

5. **How do you see your audience/customer?**

It's maturing. The public matures more quickly because it's not tied to a business objective, it's a personal use. Customers, on the other hand, take their time. They even want the service, but put the brakes on when they see that it will require more money or time to provide effective results for their cash flow.

6. **How is customer demand, what type of service is most sought after?**

There is a huge demand for content production, especially for Facebook and Instagram. This service is the easiest to sell because it's where the client actually sees the work and that's where they start looking.

The most difficult are those that involve planning, monitoring and ADS (online ads), which the client sees as practically just a PPT, the job is to show that this is important to achieve the objectives

7. How does the agency position itself in relation to market demands?

Today, the company no longer produces content; there is more competition in this area of social media. That's why it chooses to plan the digital communication and the client or another company carries it out, as well as offering the social media monitoring service.

Monitoring is an important area, but there aren't many companies (as far as I know there are only 5 in Belém: Yesbil, Life Social Web, Ovelha, Temple and Libra). So the company is ahead by offering this service.

In addition to showing through public monitoring studies, the company was the first to actually show the market how the service was done. Then the positioning came from being the first in attitude.

8. What do you think of the digital market in Belém?

In the adolescent phase of its growth. There's not as much money for the service, but there's a lot of exposure for the agencies. On the other hand, there's the client who wants to sell a stock, but social media will take six months to do so.

9. What is the agency's relationship with the public/client, how do you relate to them? Today the company relates to two audiences: students/professionals and company directors/owners. Each audience has a different content strategy.

Students demand courses and lectures, business owners demand more detailed posts and market studies. We have an e-mail base where we send different content to each audience. This helps us go beyond social networks.

10. How do you see the new consumer and how important is he for the growth and development of companies and the relationship between the public and the company/agency?

It is now possible to know who this consumer is, mainly through monitoring. We analyze who is interacting with the company to find out their habits and build products focused on them.

On the other hand, communication is learning that you can't do anything without thinking about digital, even if it's just a video that will be shown on TV. It always has implications for user behavior on the web.

If an agency doesn't see this, it will be left behind.

APPENDIX III.

Survey conducted with Josiele Soeiro, Corporate Communications and Press Office Analyst at Eko Estratégias em Comunicação (2014).

1. **What is your role within the agency? How do you work?**

I'm a corporate communications analyst and I work with the press accounts of a number of companies in Belém.

2. **What services does Eko offer? Is there a particular area of focus in the agency?**

Press relations, digital marketing, events, corporate communications, etc. For a long time, press relations was/is one of the main services offered by the company. However, with the development of a new scenario, based more on the interaction of social networks, the work of the press office has become much more integrated with Digital Marketing, making these one of the strongest areas within the company. Most of our clients keep both accounts with us. And this integration is becoming increasingly necessary.

3. **How long has the agency been in business?**

2 years.

4. **How do you see your audience/customer?**

We see every client as an opportunity. And also a constant challenge. Each client has a different profile, we work with companies from various segments ranging from the mining sector to hospitals and shopping malls, so each one has an objective ("what to communicate? To whom? In what way?). We always try to immerse ourselves in the client and read the scenario and their sector through conversations and briefings before setting the goals to be achieved through planning. Eko's role is to offer communication solutions to these companies in order to strengthen and preserve their image.

5. **How is customer demand, what type of service is most sought after?**

The demands vary greatly. Some clients require a lot of attention, every day, others not so much. Press relations is the most sought-after service, because it is this service that keeps the client in the media in a positive and "spontaneous" way. And even when there is a problem or crisis, it is the press office that mediates between the client and the press.

6. **How does the agency position itself in relation to the demands of the market?**

Eko is always attentive to changes in the scenario and the market in order to adapt more easily.

When it realizes that there are variations in communication processes, it plans a change in strategy according to each situation. The company is never against change; on the contrary, it is always looking for creative and innovative solutions.

7. What do you think of the digital market in Beiém?

It's still growing, but in recent years we've seen a vertiginous increase. More and more companies are realizing the importance of taking care of their image in the digital world. Gradually they are becoming aware that their image on the internet, especially social networks, is a serious matter that requires dedication and professional care. The possibility of crises today, with the strengthening of these networks, has greatly increased and companies like Eko have the mission of always keeping them positive with their stakeholders.

8. How does the agency relate to the public/customer? A good relationship with the client is the basis of all service at Eko. We are in direct contact with them every day. Analysts talk to their clients either by e-mail or telephone. Everything is always well aligned and approved with them. The minimum contact is a face-to-face meeting every 15 days.

9. What is your advisory work like and how important is this segment for the market and for clients?

The press office follows a plan, usually drawn up at the beginning of each year and approved by the client. It usually follows a calendar of events and stories, but it also happens that we take advantage of the scenario. The press office's work goes far beyond producing press releases or scheduling interviews: we always create opportunities so that the client is always in the media and well positioned, of course. Scenario reading is fundamental to this process. We monitor newspapers, websites, clients' competitors and business opportunities on a daily basis in order to come up with better strategies. The press office is essential for any company today, as it is responsible for keeping the client's image positive with the press and other opinion formers.

Printed by Books on Demand GmbH, Norderstedt / Germany